seven words of
WORSHIP

seven words of
WORSHIP

The Key to a Lifetime of Experiencing GOD

mike harland and stan moser

B&H
PUBLISHING GROUP
Nashville, Tennessee

978-0-8054-4758-3

Published by B&H Publishing Group,
Nashville, Tennessee

Dewey Decimal Classification: 264
Subject Heading: WORSHIP \ PUBLIC WORSHIP \ PRAISE

2 3 4 5 6 7 8 9 • 11 10 09 08

CONTENTS

LOVE

RESPONSE

EXPRESSION

PRESENCE

EXPERIENCE

FOREWORD

True worship flows from the heart in recognition of and response to the magnificence of Christ and because of an understanding of the grace found solely in the gospel. Embracing these truths through the practical experience of daily living is the key to God sending a desperately needed revival to a spiritually drifting evangelical church. It is imperative that we get this right.

Mike Harland and Stan Moser understand this reality, and they want others to understand it too, which is why I am excited about this book. It would be true to say that these two godly men are vocationally dedicated to the pursuit of meaningful worship, but to stop there would be to shortchange the work of God in their lives. Yes, they both have made important contributions through their gifts and passions for the local church, the Christian music industry, and in the area of worship music. But all that aside, they are fueled not by music in and of itself but by hearts tuned to passionate pursuit and worship of the Savior. Worship of God is woven into the fabric of their lives, and they have a passion for others to experience a deep abiding relationship with God that erupts in worshipping Him both individually and corporately for His glory.

As Christians, we do not exist to revel each Sunday in our pomp and finery. Our lives should be as worshippers of Almighty God lived as a poured-out fragrant offering before the throne. Mike and Stan eloquently and with simplicity and biblical faithfulness explain the reality of what it means to live a life as a worshipper.

There are two primary reasons we exist: to worship God and to make His name known among the nations. My prayer is that God will use *Seven Words of Worship* as a resource to draw each reader to a deeper understanding of true worship that, in turn, leads each person to a desire to see Christ exalted among the nations that the world's peoples might know the joy of worship as well.

—Thom S. Rainer
President and CEO
LifeWay Christian Resources

PREFACE

When the invitation came, I was absolutely certain that I wasn't ready. To be honest with you, it just didn't make any sense to my natural mind. Somehow, some way, I was supposed to write a book on experiencing God in worship.

I spent most of the day arguing with God. Surely He was calling the wrong guy this time. Don't get me wrong; a book to encourage and empower people to experience God in worship certainly is a good idea. After all, most of us want a deeper encounter with God, don't we? Well, at least we like the idea.

I told God that He really should invite some well-known author, worship leader, or eloquent speaker to take on the task. In fact, I spent quite a bit of time that day mulling over the list of prominent worship leaders who would be perfect for the job. Yes, that was it: I could plant the idea for this book with one of them, and they would jump at the opportunity.

I went to bed that night quite confident that I had found the solution. I had spent my entire adult life working with the most prominent artists, writers, and communicators in the church today. All I had to do was "help God" find the right one. What a relief.

The alarm went off at 5:00 a.m.—not the one on the nightstand, but the one in my head. I didn't hear an audible voice, but God's command was quite clear, "Get up and write." Now that may sound strange to you. But I've "heard" that voice before, and I knew it was crucial to respond.

Before long I was sitting in the living room, yellow pad in hand, and seven words came to mind. I wrote them down. Frankly, they are pretty common words—*creation, love, grace, response, expression, presence,* and *experience.* Not terribly inspiring words on the surface, but absolutely life-changing words when put in context.

As the Lord linked them together over the next hour, I began to realize that these simple words just might be the key that allows many ordinary people like you and me to experience God in new and powerful ways. That simple message just might be the key to unlocking a new level of freedom in worship allowing us to become "portals of His presence" to those around us. That these seven words just might be the keys to a lifetime of experiencing God.

One year later, when I met Mike Harland, God made it clear that he was indeed that "well-known worship leader and speaker" who would help bring these words of worship to life for you and me. I assure you, Mike's insights and life experiences will inspire you to pursue a worship lifestyle and experience God in your own life like never before.

If there is that place of longing and hunger for more of God's presence in your life—this book is for you. If you are one who really does want to worship God in spirit and in truth, but you aren't sure what that means—this book is for you.

God has promised His presence when we worship Him. He wants you to *break through* the doubts and traditions that have held you back. And He is ready to *break in* to every *broken* place in your life. It really is that simple: God inhabits the praises of His people. And when the King is present, all things are possible.

So come with expectation as you read. Look diligently into God's Word with us, and you will see His face—you will know His presence. These seven simple words really can be your keys to a lifetime of experiencing God in worship. The time for your break through is right now. This invitation is for you.

—Stan Moser

When I came to LifeWay nearly three years ago, I had a burning mission in my heart and a recurring prayer. *"God, favor my work so that I can share the message about worship You have put in my heart."* I didn't know then, nor do I know now, all the ways God will answer that prayer. But I believe one of those ways is this book, *Seven Words of Worship.*

I will be forever grateful for my friend and coauthor Stan Moser for the energy and insights he brought to this message. It is amazing how God brought us together from such different experiences; yet we found unity and agreement around this message. Only God's Word can do that and I give God glory for that unity.

My desire for this project is that it will turn your focus away from us, away from music, and even away from worship itself. Let me explain:

I have often told my choirs and churches that if people left our services saying, "What an awesome choir" or "That's a great church," then we have failed in our mission. No, the only thing I want said is, "What an awesome God!"

I feel the same way about this book. If all you get here is an impression of this book and the two authors, or even the message of worship it contains, then we have failed. I am concerned whenever I hear someone say, "You ought to experience the worship at our church—it's awesome!" I'm afraid when we say that, we reveal that our worship is the point. This book is not about experiencing *worship*, it's about experiencing *God*. If we do that, our worship will be the natural result.

If there is anything of eternal value here, it is because of the eternal value of God's Word.

I give Him glory for who He is and what He has done in my life, and I thank Him for my wife, Teresa, and our children, Lee, Elizabeth, and John, who have shown me so much love.

—Mike Harland

Introduction

But an hour is coming, and is now here, when the true worshipers will worship the Father in spirit and truth. Yes, the Father wants such people to worship Him.

(JOHN 4:23)

There is a deep and growing interest in worship these days, and that makes perfect sense. After all, worship is the primary reason we come together as the body of Christ each week. We gather to focus our attention and energy on giving glory to God; and when we do, we encounter God in powerful, life-changing ways. We are challenged and empowered to join God as He works in the world.

There are many forms of worship and certainly many different styles of worship. The body of Christ is a broad, diverse family, and the forms of our worship can often cause confusion and division. God is never the author of confusion, and His Word gives clear guidelines that empower and liberate all believers in their worship expressions. Authentic worship is simply a genuine expression of praise, adoration, celebration, and thanksgiving to God in response to who He is and what He has done in our lives.

The book you are holding explores what it means for us as the body of Christ and as individuals, including how to pursue authentic worship—not only in our weekly worship services, but also in our everyday lives. You will be introduced to *seven words of worship* that will serve as

1

a guide for *knowing* and *experiencing* God in worship. As you apply these teachings in your own life, you will be inspired and equipped to develop a *lifestyle of worship,* which is God's desire for every believer.

We are passionate about helping individuals and congregations develop a consistent lifestyle of worship. As you increase in understanding of who God is and what He has done in your life, consistent and fervent worship will be your natural response. And as you worship, God will inhabit your praise and impact your circumstances.

Our Threefold Purpose

Seven Words of Worship was initiated by God and birthed through years of effort by my coauthor and friend, Stan Moser. Although this is a collaborative work, I (Mike) will serve as the "voice" throughout this book, representing our collective insights that we pray will accomplish our threefold purpose:

1. To help you gain a clear revelation of God who desires worship to be the focal point and passion of our lives (Rom. 12:1);
2. To give you a solid understanding of the biblical foundation that leads us to become true worshippers (John 4:23–24); and
3. To encourage you to enter into biblical authenticity in your worship as you respond to God's revelation evidenced in your daily expression of faith in Christ (2 Cor. 3:17).

About This Book

To achieve these goals, we present some simple, foundational truths about biblical worship in eight sections with five chapters in each section. This format allows you to read and embrace the content over a forty-day period.

Each section combines biblical insights with real-life stories and personal reflections that are designed to help you apply what you are reading. Though you may sense a logical progression in the core concepts, we will explore them from different angles and consider subtle nuances to maximize your understanding and application. There will be several key Scriptures in each section to reinforce biblical truths central to your study and to help hide God's Word in your heart.

Music and Worship Go Hand in Hand

Each section of this book begins with a "Song of Worship" that may or may not be familiar to you. We encourage you to read and meditate on the lyrics. The lyrics will speak directly to your heart, inspiring your own expression of praise to God. The CD, *Words of Worship . . . for a Lifetime of Experiencing God,* is designed to enhance your reading experience. To purchase go to www.lifeway.com or your local Christian retailer.

Here are a few suggestions that will help bring this book to life for you:

- Trust the Holy Spirit to be your teacher. Ask Him for guidance as you seek to gain greater biblical understanding of authentic worship and develop your lifestyle of worship. Release your mind and heart in ready obedience to all He will teach you.
- Be consistent—a lifestyle of worship is a radical change for many, and diligent attention to the Word of God is the key.
- Take time each day to express your worship and appreciation to the King of kings.
- Pray for revelation and breakthrough.

As you read, our hope and prayer is that you will be filled with a refreshing and clear perspective of authentic worship, and you will be challenged to fulfill God's desire for you to lift your voice and your *life* as an expression of worship.

THE HEART
OF WORSHIP

Song of Worship

"Unto the One"

You broke the curse of sin
You were slain Lamb of God
No greater love has ever been displayed
Crucified at the hands of sinners You were
Risen to life on the third day

Victorious One, Great Healer
You are worthy, Jesus worthy
There is no end to Your majesty
Lamb of God, You bought with Your blood
Men from every tribe and tongue
Lion of Judah, You have overcome

(Chorus)
Unto the One who sits on the throne
Unto the Lamb who was slain
Be all blessing and honor
Glory and power and praise forever

(Bridge)
Worthy is the Lamb of God
Who takes away the sins of the world

—WORDS AND MUSIC BY MATT PAPA
COPYRIGHT 2005 SPIN SONGS, ADMIN. BY MARANATHA! MUSIC, AND
MARANATHA! MUSIC (ADMIN. BY MUSIC SERVICES, NASHVILLE)

1

Experiencing God— A Personal Encounter

Worship is the key to experiencing God in our lives.

There is a real hunger in the church today to know and experience God in a personal way. Truth is, we were created to know God in this way, to have a relationship with Him. God made us this way because He desired an intimate relationship with us before the beginning of time.

God Desires a Relationship with Us

All lasting relationships are based on mutual interest, trust, and understanding. By choosing to create us in His image—with a mind (the ability to reason), a will, and emotions—and by providing everything we need for life, God created and equipped us for a lasting relationship with Him.

My brother, Bill, is my "big brother" in every sense of the word. Not only is he three years older than me, but he was always much bigger than me. He was what they called "an early bloomer," always the biggest boy in his class. He was a good athlete and often the captain of whatever game was going on. Two things were true when it came to Bill and me: he picked on me all the time and he made sure that absolutely no one else did. One day in the 5th grade I learned the advantages of having a brother like Bill. I was walking toward the cafeteria when two 7th graders stopped me and demanded my milk money. I felt like I had no choice but to dig down in my pocket and give it to them. I had just handed it over when a friend of the two walked by and said, "What are you doing? Don't you know who that is? That's Bill Harland's little brother." Immediately they gave me my money back! I was never happier to be Bill Harland's little brother.

When it comes to worship, it's all about relationship—relationship with God through His Son, Jesus Christ. I did nothing to get my milk money back that day except be Bill's little brother. In the same way, we've done nothing to deserve a worship encounter with the Living God, except receiving the redemption found only in Jesus.

From beginning to end, the Bible makes it clear that God desires a relationship with us. He wants us to know who He is, who we are in relationship to Him, how we should respond, and what we can expect in return. As we examine these aspects of God's desire and plan for relationship with us, consider what the following verses tell us:

> *Where can I go to escape Your Spirit?*
> *Where can I flee from Your presence?*
> *If I go up to heaven, You are there;*
> *If I make my bed in Sheol, You are there. (Ps. 139:7–8)*

> *"I am the vine; you are the branches. The one who remains in Me and I in him produces much fruit, because you can do nothing without Me." (John 15:5)*

> *"In a little while the world will see Me no longer, but you will see Me. Because I live, you will live too. In that day you will know that I am in My Father, you are in Me, and I am in you." (John 14:19–20)*

> *This is how we know that we remain in Him and He in us: He has given to us from His Spirit. And we have seen and we testify that the Father has sent the Son as Savior of the world. Whoever confesses that Jesus is the Son of God— God remains in him and he in God. (1 John 4:13–15)*

These four passages of Scripture leave no room for doubt: God loves us and desires a personal relationship with each of us. All we have to do is respond! God wants to reveal Himself and His will in every situation of our lives. As we respond, we can experience God every day.

Worship Is the Key to Experiencing God

A number of years ago, Henry Blackaby and Claude King provided us with wonderful insights and principles on how to experience God and discover His will in our everyday lives. Their best-selling book *Experiencing God* gave us clear instruction to help us fulfill our purpose on the earth: see what God is doing around us and join Him as He works through us. It all begins with God's offer of a personal and intimate relationship. As we respond, we really can experience God!

Experiencing God delivered a tried and proven message for the church, and I've seen the results in an up-close-and-personal way. You see, I've spent my entire adult life serving in churches, from some of the smallest to the largest churches in America, and I've seen many of God's people embrace His mission for their lives—the plans God prepared for them before they were even born. I've also seen many others miss their opportunity to experience God.

For years I wondered what it would take for more of God's church—ordinary folks like you and me—to fully embrace His love for us, step beyond our distractions and doubts, and truly join God as He works right where we live. *I believe with all my heart that the key to breakthrough—the key to experiencing God in our own lives and having a personal relationship with Him—is found in developing a lifestyle of worship.*

Worship Is Our Response to God's Revelation

Throughout this book, we will use this working definition of *worship:*

Worship is our response to God's revelation of who He is and what He has done.

But we have to be careful that what we are responding to is, in fact, God's revelation. We are so prone to trust our own perception and emotion that we can substitute them for reality in a heartbeat.

One day God gave me a real-life illustration of my tendency to do that very thing.

I was flying from Nashville to Dallas and was already in my seat when a smartly dressed professional lady boarded the plane and took the seat across the aisle from me. I attempted to speak to her but received no response. *She's a little rude,* I thought to myself. Throughout the flight I noticed her preoccupation with her laptop. She wouldn't even respond to the flight attendant when asked if she wanted a drink. I kept right on sizing her up. *Boy, she thinks she's really important. I wonder what her problem is.*

When we landed at DFW, she immediately took out her cell phone and fired it up. This was before the airlines would let you do that and my "judgment meter" was really in full gear now. This is when the Lord reeled my flesh right on in for the kill. *Well, look at that. She thinks she's so important that the rules don't apply to her. It's not like she's a surgeon and she's flying in to do emergency surgery in a life-or-death matter.* I had no more finished that thought when the person she was calling answered the phone and she said, "I've just landed. Is the patient prepped for surgery? I've been reviewing the procedure on the flight. Is the police escort going to meet me at the gate or in front of the airport? I should be there in twenty minutes. Every moment will count." When we got to the gate, she was escorted off the plane by an agent and whisked away to try and save someone's life. I started to cry as I asked the Lord to forgive me and then prayed for her and the person she would be operating on in just minutes.

Since we are so prone to be presumptuous all the time, we better be sure where we look for information about our God when we gather to worship Him. And God has faithfully given us ways to know who He is so that we can be confident when we worship Him.

Simply stated, we are called to respond to all that God has revealed about Himself and to His never-ending desire to enter a deeper relationship with each of us. Through the ages God has been in the constant process of revealing His character and essence. Yes, God is mysterious in many ways, but He is never a mystery. He has gone to great lengths to reveal Himself throughout history—including sending His Son, Jesus, into the world—and He continues to reveal Himself today in at least three ways:

1. God reveals Himself in creation.
2. God reveals Himself through His Word.
3. God reveals Himself through the Holy Spirit.

God created us for relationship with Him and deeply desires to reveal Himself—who He is and what He has done—to us. He has promised to meet us as we worship. In fact, as we understand and embrace all that God has done for us in Christ Jesus, our only reasonable and adequate response is worship. Our response to God always requires faith and corresponding action, yet God never forces us to respond—it is always *our* choice.

Worship Invites God's Presence

God deeply desires a personal relationship with each one of us, and He is at work around us at all times. Just as God walked and talked with Adam and Eve in the garden of Eden, so He desires to fellowship and communicate with each of us. God has promised in Psalm 22:3 to inhabit the praises of His people, and God is always true to His promises. Our worship provides a place of meeting with God—a place for us to encounter His very presence and embrace His invitation to join Him as He works.

> But You are holy, O You Who dwell in [the holy place where] the praises of Israel [are offered]. (Ps. 22:3 AMP)

As we focus our time and attention on the Lord in worship, proclaim His place of honor in our lives, and thank and praise Him for His eternal promises, we can expect God to intervene in our circumstances. God has promised to inhabit our worship, and He *will*. And when the King is present, all things are possible!

> Enter His gates with thanksgiving, and His courts with praise. Give thanks to Him and praise His name. For the LORD is good, and His love is eternal; His faithfulness endures through all generations. (Ps. 100:4–5)

That's why we must worship through the good times and the bad— when we're waiting for God's merciful touch in our circumstances and when we're standing in awe of His power at work around us. Worship invites God's presence, enabling us to experience God.

The Bible is filled with many examples of those who responded to God's revelation with worship and experienced Him. You'll find their names throughout Scripture—Abraham, David, Daniel and his friends, Mary, Joseph, Peter, and Paul. As you read further, you will soon understand how absolutely vital worship was in their lives.

These great Bible heroes had a clear revelation of God—of who He is and what He has done. They responded to that revelation with worship, and they experienced the presence and power of God in their lives. Their lives are confirmation: *you and I can experience God in worship!*

Psalm 22:3 is a cornerstone verse on worship. It is often helpful to look at a passage of Scripture in different translations to fully grasp the meaning of each word or phrase.

> *But thou art holy,*
> *O thou that inhabitest the praises of Israel. (Ps. 22:3 KJV)*
>
> *But You are holy,*
> *enthroned on the praises of Israel. (Ps. 22:3 HCSB)*
>
> *But You are holy, O You Who dwell in [the holy place where]*
> *the praises of Israel [are offered]. (Ps. 22:3 AMP)*

Let's take a look at the meaning of several key words in that passage from the King James Version, the Holman Christian Standard Bible, the Amplified Bible (see above) or your favorite translation.

Holy—sacred, spiritually pure, sinless, deserving deep respect and awe

Inhabit—to live in

Enthroned—placed on a throne and exalted

Our God does indeed deserve our deep respect, awe, and worship! And He has promised His holy presence as we worship. Simply put, our worship expression creates a *place* for us to encounter and experience God.

Think about It This Way

When we think about worship, we often think about what we receive from the experience. But what about what God receives?

Our daughter Elizabeth is the second child of three and our only girl. I often tell people, "We have three children—one of each." What I mean is that each one is so different from the other two—in personality, in strengths and interests—that they seem like three different kinds of people! Recently Elizabeth and I went on a college visit together. She is a senior right now and selecting where she will go to college is a real priority for us. As we were driving, we began to talk about life at our house after Elizabeth goes to college. I can tell you, I'm not looking forward to it. I've already sent one off to college—my son Lee, and that was hard. But sending Elizabeth off to school feels very different and, to be honest, I dread it. You see, Elizabeth is a big part of our family "sound track." You know what a family "sound track" is, don't you? That's what your family sounds like when you are all there. Our son Lee is on the quiet side and is very happy in his room listening to a symphony or something. Sometimes we don't even know he's there. But Elizabeth (I call her "Little B") is usually with us unfolding the latest drama of her life in full detail.

As we were driving toward the college, it hit me how much quieter our "sound track" will be when she leaves for school. We will still have plenty of stuff to do to keep us busy and places to go with John still at home—plenty of everything, except Elizabeth. And, in the words of Bob Benson—noted music publisher, author, and speaker—in "parental math," busy minus Elizabeth won't equal plenty. Soon the tears began to flow as I started missing my "Little B."

I'm convinced God feels that way about us, too. I remember singing tenor in a choir with a bunch of great (and loud) tenors recently and feeling like I wasn't needed. Just as I was thinking to myself, *They don't need me. I might as well not sing in this choir,* I sensed a nudge from the Holy Spirit say, "Sing for Me! I want to hear you sing because no one can take your place with Me!" I started singing again as strong as I could!

God has plenty of everything—except you. And your worship is the time when you open up yourself and pour out on the One who loves you more than anyone else. So, don't always be consumed with what you *get* in worship. Think about what you *give.* God wants worship from *you.* No one else can give that to Him.

Call to Worship

As you read this book, I encourage you to offer up your own unique expression of worship—an expression of appreciation, adoration, desperation, and expectation that is reserved deep within you for God and God alone. Whether your worship includes three verses and a chorus, liturgical litanies, *a cappella* hymns, banners and dance, solemn assembly, or loud, exuberant praise, God is waiting to hear from you.

And as you respond to His great love and sacrifice for you—whether you are worshipping corporately or in the privacy of your own home—you *will* experience God. He is ready, willing, and able to meet you right where you are as you enter into worship.

Reflections

- God desires a personal relationship with each of us.
- Worship is our response to God's revelation of who He is and what He has done.
- Our worship creates a place to encounter God's presence and embrace His invitation to join Him as He works.
- God has promised to inhabit our praises as we worship Him.
- God wants to hear our personal expressions of worship.
- Worship is the key to experiencing God in our lives!

Prayer

Dear Father, thank You for loving me and for making a way for me to know You. God, open my eyes so I can see Your greatness. Give me a hunger for Your Word and a desire to give You my worship as long as I live! Amen.

God's Revelation and Our Response

Worship is our only reasonable response to God's revelation.

In *Experiencing God,* Henry Blackaby and Claude King suggest there are seven realities in the process of experiencing God:

1. God is always at work around you.
2. God pursues a continuing love relationship with you that is real and personal.
3. God invites you to become involved with Him in His work.
4. God speaks by the Holy Spirit through the Bible, prayer, circumstances, and the church to reveal Himself, His purposes, and His ways.
5. God's invitation for you to work with Him always leads you to a crisis of belief that requires faith and action.
6. You must make major adjustments in your life to join God in what He is doing.
7. You come to know God by experience as you obey Him and He accomplishes His work through you.[1]

If you, like millions of other believers, have chosen to join God as He is working around and through you, then you know what experiencing God is all about. The message of *Experiencing God* is not just a good idea; it is a powerful guideline for all believers. God always wants to reach you and use you to impact those around you. I have discovered in my own life that worship is an integral part of this process.

A Personal "Experiencing God" Story

My journey to become Director of the Worship Department at LifeWay Christian Resources is a good example of the link between worship and experiencing God. Just a few years ago, I was the worship leader and music minister at First Baptist Church in Carrollton, Texas. My wife, Teresa, and I were so happy there—the friends and church family God gave us in Texas had become home for us and our three children. My role at the church was fulfilling in every way.

But God . . . ! Have you ever encountered those two words in your own life? We truly loved our time in Texas. It was a great place to live, and we were surrounded by some of the most wonderful people God ever created. *But God* began to invite me to join Him in a new work at LifeWay. I still remember the day He made His invitation completely clear.

I had arrived at LifeWay Conference Center in Ridgecrest, North Carolina, for my final round of interviews with LifeWay leadership. In the midst of the first evening there, I found myself wandering through the empty two-thousand-seat auditorium—just me and God in a darkened sanctuary that had been home to the heartfelt sounds of worship for so many over the years.

As I walked across the stage, it occurred to me that I had been on that very stage twenty-seven years earlier when, as a sixteen-year-old boy, I was selected to perform one of the first songs I had written in an evening worship service. Although I hadn't been back to that auditorium in all those years, I vividly remembered the excitement and anxiety of that moment. I thought about how small the auditorium looked to me after all these years journeying from my small church in north Mississippi to some of the largest churches in America. I realized that God had been with me all along the way and that He could see this day of decision on that day so many years before. He had faithfully guided my life all the days in between—leading me to this very opportunity to join Him in a new ministry effort.

God was with me on that stage that night, just as He had been with me in that very spot twenty-seven years earlier. The intimidated sixteen-year-old boy had become a grown man who was still filled with adolescent excitement and anxiety at the possibility of leading my denomination's worship efforts.

At that moment, I knew. I had a clear revelation of God's desire for me to step out of my comfort zone in Carrollton, Texas, and join Him as He impacts the worship life of believers across the globe. I surrendered to God's call and began to weep as I sang out loud:

If You can use anything, Lord, You can use me,
If You can use anything, Lord, You can use me.[2]

On that cool April evening in Ridgecrest, North Carolina, I sensed God's presence so strong and understood clearly the invitation to join Him in His work at LifeWay. As I sang, I surrendered my will and experienced God in worship.

My journey to serve at LifeWay had begun. Over the next few weeks, my wife, Teresa, and I worked through the inevitable crisis of belief that always comes as we respond to God's invitation—when doubts and questions creep in and we must make major adjustments in our lives in order to be obedient to God. We planned our move and put our faith in His call into action. God had revealed Himself and directed our steps once again. Joining Him as He works is the ultimate experience in life!

Do you have an "experiencing God" story to tell—a story of a time when you experienced God's presence and call to join Him in His work? If you don't have an experiencing God story yet, don't be discouraged. Just spend some time asking God to show you how He is at work around you, and He will. God deeply desires to reveal more of Himself and His activities to you because He truly loves you. God wants a real, personal relationship with you above all else. And He wants to reveal Himself to you in real, tangible ways.

Take a few minutes to contemplate each of the following descriptions about God and His activities in your life. If you question any of these statements, go directly to the Scripture referenced and confirm what God's Word clearly says about His character and His actions.

Who God Is	**What God Has Done**
God Almighty (Gen. 17:1)	Created the earth and everything in it (Gen. 1)
Prince of Peace (Isa. 9:6)	Overcame the enemy (Col. 2:15)
King of kings (Rev. 19:16)	Died for our sins and iniquities (Rom. 8:3–4)
Lord of all (Acts 10:36)	Chose to dwell with us and in us (John 16:7; 1 Cor. 6:19)
Savior (1 Tim. 4:10)	Loved us with an everlasting love (John 3:16)
Redeemer (Titus 2:14)	Justified us (Rom. 5:18)
Counselor (John 14:26)	Called us His children (Rom. 8:16–17)
Friend (James 2:23)	Gave us new life (Rom. 6:4)
Healer (Isa. 53:4–5)	Set us free (Heb. 2:14–15)
Our Righteousness (Jer. 23:6)	Made us righteous (2 Cor. 5:21)
Our Security (Ps. 91)	Gave us authority (Mark 16:15–18)
Comforter (2 Cor. 1:3)	Forgave us (1 John 1:9)

Call to Worship

God is the great King of kings. He has given us everything we need for life and godliness. He is our Provider, our Salvation, our Strength. He is our All in All. And He is waiting for you to respond to who He is and what He has done!

As you continue to read, you will see more clearly that worship is your only reasonable and adequate response to God's revelation. Regardless of your current or past circumstances, you have so many compelling reasons to set aside all else and worship Him. Your "*experiencing God*" story is on the way!

Reflections

- God has promised to be present as we worship.
- As we experience God in worship, we open ourselves to hear His call.
- Worship always evokes a response to join God in His work.
- God's invitation to join Him as He works requires faith and action, adjustments and obedience.
- We must be careful that our impressions of God are based on His revelation and not our perceptions and emotions.

- The Bible gives clear revelation of who God is and what He has done. As we accept and believe this revelation, our natural response is to worship Him!

Prayer

Lord Jesus, thank You for Your presence. Give me the wisdom to trust Your revelation and not just my impressions. Let my service grow out of my worship instead of simply following a ritual and expecting Your blessing. Amen.

Notes

1. Henry Blackaby and Claude King, *Experiencing God* (Nashville: Broadman & Holman Publishers, 1994), 52–64.

2. "Use Me" by Dewitt Jones, ©1993 Deinde Music/BMI (adm by Integrity's Praise! Music) & Integrity's Praise! Music/BMI, c/o Intregity Media, Inc., 1000 Cody Road, Mobile, AL 36695.

3

Free to Worship

We are free to worship God because of Jesus' sacrifice.

In spite of all the reasons we have been given to worship God, He still gives us the freedom to choose whether or not we will express our worship. He knows that worshipping the invisible God does not come naturally to us. In our human condition, we are more inclined to turn our affections toward something or someone we can see, touch, understand, and control. We are more likely to worship carnal things. That was certainly the case for God's people in the day of Moses:

> The LORD spoke to Moses: "Go down at once! For your people you brought up from the land of Egypt have acted corruptly. They have quickly turned from the way I commanded them; they have made for themselves an image of a calf. They have bowed down to it, sacrificed to it, and said, 'Israel, this is your God, who brought you up from the land of Egypt.'" (Exod. 32:7–8)

The Israelites were so desperate to have a tangible experience with God that, even while Moses was on Mount Sinai meeting with the great

I AM, they crafted a counterfeit image to worship. In this act of disobedience, they demonstrated not only their very deep, human need to
experience the presence of God, but also mankind's natural inclination
to meet that need in an illegitimate manner.

Preparation—A Matter of Life and Death

In Moses' day God's presence was not always available to every person. It was dangerous to encounter God's holy presence without appropriate preparation. The priests were the ones who had access to God's
presence, and their preparation to meet with God was literally a matter
of life and death. That preparation was detailed and meticulous. Even
the holiest priests could not survive an encounter with the one and only
righteous and holy God without appropriate cleansing and sacrifice.

The priests were required to:

- be consecrated in a specific manner to serve as priests
  (see Exod. 29:1–46; Lev. 8:1–36);
- wear the sacred garments whenever they entered the
  tabernacle of meeting so they wouldn't incur guilt and die
  (see Exod. 28:2–43);
- burn fragrant incense on the altar every morning and evening
  (see Exod. 30:7–8);
- wash their hands and feet with water from the sacred basin
  (see Exod. 30:19–21); and
- make atonement annually with the blood of the sin offering
  for atonement (see Exod. 30:10).

There was a stiff penalty for the priests if they did not comply with
these regulations. For example, in Leviticus 8 we see that Aaron and his
sons were ordained as priests and did everything just right. In Leviticus
9 they launched their ministries. However, in chapter 10 they missed
the mark, and God literally sent fire to consume two of Aaron's sons,
removing them from the ministry!

Aaron survived his sons' mistakes, but only after God provided a
way out of their disobedience. God provided what became known as
the Day of Atonement. Of course, that meant there were more rules and
regulations that had to be followed on this special day in order for the
priests to enter God's presence (see Lev. 16).

I was living in Austin, Texas, and serving at Hyde Park Baptist Church
when George W. Bush became the 43rd President of the United States.

Several members of our church served on his campaign staff and subsequently joined his White House staff when he moved to Washington. Because of one of those friends in particular, I've since had the opportunity to go to the White House five or six times. In the summer of 2005, I took my parents as a part of celebrating their 50th wedding anniversary. On that visit I made a mistake that could have given me a free afternoon with the Secret Service if I had not realized it when I did.

My friend had arranged for my parents and me to gain access to the South Lawn for a Marine One departure of the President, something I had actually done twice before on previous visits. The only difference this time was my friend was out of town and would not be escorting us. He had arranged for one of his interns to meet us at the security gate and escort us through the Rose Garden to the South Lawn. We arrived early and went right through security with no problem. Our names were on the list since we had submitted our personal information weeks before in anticipation of this possibility. The intern had not arrived yet and we were waiting when I suddenly had a less-than-brilliant idea. Since I thought I knew my way around a little bit, I decided to take my mom and dad on a little sightseeing tour of the White House grounds. We had drifted all the way out to the front lawn when suddenly I had this terrifying realization. *We had clearance to be there, but we were admitted only as visitors and visitors can only be there under escort of staff.* I was walking around like I owned the place, but I had no business being where I was.

I calmly suggested to my parents that we might want to move back toward the gate and wait for the intern. It was then I noticed about half a dozen pairs of eyes watching our every move. I got real humble, real fast.

It occurs to me that we sometimes approach our worship encounters of Holy God with the same presumption. We are there only by virtue of our escort, Jesus Himself. It seems the holiness of His presence can be so familiar to us that we lose the respect of where we are and how we got there. We rush onto the front lawn when we ought to be waiting at the gate and waiting for His guidance into the presence of our Sovereign God.

The Perfect Sacrifice

There just had to be a better way for God's people to enter His presence—and there was! Everything changed when God made the supreme sacrifice in Christ Jesus. Through His life, death, and resurrection, we have been given freedom to enter God's presence:

> Now the Messiah has appeared, high priest of the good
> things that have come. In the greater and more perfect
> tabernacle not made with hands (that is, not of this creation),
> He entered the holy of holies once for all, not by the blood
> of goats and calves, but by His own blood, having obtained
> eternal redemption. For if the blood of goats and bulls and
> the ashes of a heifer sprinkling those who are defiled, sanctify
> for the purification of the flesh, how much more will the blood
> of the Messiah, who through the eternal Spirit offered Himself
> without blemish to God, cleanse our consciences from dead
> works to serve the living God? (Heb. 9:11–14)

Now it is no longer necessary for God's people to send a representative or priest to enter the holy of holies—the place where God resides. There is no need for the veil of separation to protect us from His glorious presence. There is no need for us to wait for some contemporary Moses to "come down from the mountain." By the blood of Jesus, the perfect sacrifice, we have been made righteous—worthy to encounter God personally.

The Bible clearly indicates that no one is able to come to the Father on his or her own merit:

> "There is no one righteous, not even one;" . . . For all have
> sinned and fall short of the glory of God. (Rom. 3:10, 23)

None of us is righteous of our own accord. But through the loving sacrifice of Christ Jesus, we have been made righteous. To consider ourselves anything other than righteous and worthy of the presence of God disagrees with what God has said and done.

> He made the One who did not know sin to be sin for us,
> so that we might become the righteousness of God in Him.
> (2 Cor. 5:21)

Based on what you know about your own activities and actions throughout your life, is it hard for you to accept that you are righteous? If God's sacrifice of His own dear Son was not enough to cover your sins and make you worthy of His presence, is there something else that you can do? In light of 2 Corinthians 5:21, what would it take for you to be convinced that you are righteous in God's sight?

Slaves to Righteousness and Free to Worship!

God's answer to the previous three questions for those who have accepted Jesus as Lord and Savior is *absolutely nothing!* By faith in Christ Jesus, you are no longer a slave to sin but have been set free from sin and have become a slave to righteousness.

> *And having been liberated from sin, you became enslaved to righteousness. (Rom. 6:18)*

A slave simply has no choice—he or she must obey the master. Before Jesus redeemed our lives, sin was our master. But now we have a new Master, and as the Scriptures affirm, we can live a righteous life that He alone provides and requires.

> *For just as through one man's disobedience the many were made sinners, so also through the one man's obedience the many will be made righteous. (Rom. 5:19)*

If you have been living under condemnation for your sins, past or present, now is the time to believe the Word of God and gain victory over sin and self-condemnation. The apostle Paul explains it this way:

> *Therefore, no condemnation now exists for those in Christ Jesus, because the Spirit's law of life in Christ Jesus has set you free from the law of sin and of death. What the law could not do since it was limited by the flesh, God did. He condemned sin in the flesh by sending His own Son in flesh like ours under sin's domain, and as a sin offering, in order that the law's requirement would be accomplished in us who do not walk according to the flesh but according to the Spirit. (Rom. 8:1–4)*

Now is the time to confess what God says about you, not what your mind and emotions have been telling you. As you confess or speak God's Word, it will take root in your heart by faith and change the way you think and act. You do not have to live by what you see or be moved by what you feel.

Believing what God says rather than what you think or feel is an act of your will. You are free to worship God because Jesus paid the price for your transgressions. You are free to worship because He says you are!

Call to Worship

Take a look at each of the following Scriptures. As you understand these promises and receive them personally, you will find new freedom in worship!

> *Therefore, no condemnation now exists for those in Christ Jesus, because the Spirit's law of life in Christ Jesus has set you free from the law of sin and of death. (Rom. 8:1–2)*

Condemnation as used here comes from a legal term referring to a verdict of guilty and the penalty that verdict demands. As a believer, no sin you commit—past, present, or future—can be held against you, since the penalty was paid in full by Christ and righteousness has been imputed to you.

> *Now the Lord is the Spirit; and where the Spirit of the Lord is, there is freedom. We all, with unveiled faces, are reflecting the glory of the Lord and are being transformed into the same image from glory to glory; this is from the Lord who is the Spirit. (2 Cor. 3:17–18)*

When you accept Jesus as Lord and Savior, you receive the indwelling Holy Spirit. The Holy Spirit liberates every captive of sin, including you and me. As you focus your heart and mind on Jesus, the Spirit transforms you more and more into His image—from one level of glory to another. As you surrender every part of your life to Him, you can come boldly before God and worship Him with a pure heart.

Reflections

- God gives us the freedom to choose whether or not we will worship Him.
- Worshipping the invisible God does not come naturally to us. As humans, we are likely to worship someone or something we can see or touch.
- In Moses' day, only Moses and those consecrated as priests could enter God's presence. Any failure on their part to properly prepare could result in death.
- Our sin, which separates us from a holy, righteous God, makes us unworthy of God's presence.

- God sent Jesus to provide the way for all believers to enter God's presence. Through His shed blood on the cross, we have been made righteous.
- Nothing other than faith in Jesus is necessary for each of us to enter the presence of God!
- We should enter His presence with humility and wonder.

Prayer

Lord, make me sensitive to those things in my life that would hinder my worship of You. Forgive me for taking Your holiness too lightly. Bring to my mind those sins and attitudes that would separate me from Your power. Give me clean hands and a pure heart as I bow in reverence before You now. Amen.

4

God Inhabits
Our Worship

When we worship, God has promised to be present.

God is at work around you right now, and He wants a deep personal relationship with you. A very important key to that relationship is having a correct view of God in relationship to mankind. Throughout the ages, God has been in the continual process of revealing to us His character and His essence. Almost everyone on planet Earth believes in some kind of god; and our God, the great I AM, has gone to great lengths to reveal Himself to us through creation, through His Word (both the written Word and the Living Word, Jesus Christ), and through the Holy Spirit.

> *From the creation of the world His invisible attributes, that is, His eternal power and divine nature, have been clearly seen, being understood through what He has made. As a result, people are without excuse. (Rom. 1:20)*
> *He is the image of the invisible God. (Col. 1:15)*

*"In the beginning was the Word, and the Word was with
God, and the Word was God. . . . The Word became flesh
and took up residence among us." (John 1:1, 14)*

*When the Spirit of truth comes, He will guide you into all the
truth. For He will not speak on His own, but He will speak
whatever He hears. He will also declare to you what is to
come. He will glorify Me, because He will take from what
is Mine and declare it to you. Everything the Father has is
Mine. This is why I told you that He takes from what is Mine
and will declare it to you. (John 16:13–15)*

God has revealed and *continues to reveal* Himself to us—who He
is and what He has done—and His presence is real and available to us
today. Worship is our only reasonable response to God's revelation!

Worship Invites the Presence of God

We were created to have a relationship with God and to respond to
His great love for us with worship. And something wonderful happens
as we worship: we make a place for God to dwell in our midst. When we
worship, we actually invite the presence of God to be manifest among
us:

*But You are holy, O You Who dwell in [the holy place where]
the praises of Israel [are offered]. (Ps. 22:3 AMP)*

As we spend time in God's presence, He directs us and empowers
us to respond, and we experience Him in new and glorious ways.

Abraham is an example of a man who spent time worshipping
God—inviting God's presence. Throughout his journey from his childhood home in Ur to his season of failure in Egypt, Abraham met regularly with God, experienced God's presence, and faithfully responded
to God's direction. When he ultimately received the promise—his dear
son, Isaac—he must have thought his journey of faith was fulfilled. But
God had further revelation and breakthrough planned for Abraham's
life. (To read more about Abraham, see Gen. 12:7; 13:14–15; 15:4–6,
18; 17:1–3; 18:1.)

One day God called Abraham to literally sacrifice Isaac—the
child of promise, the joy of his life, and the hope for future generations. Abraham was empowered by God to climb Mount Moriah and
place Isaac on the altar. Abraham's response to God's revelation was

worship—and God responded! God inhabited Abraham's worship, Isaac was spared, and Abraham experienced God.

> *"Take your son," He said, "your only son Isaac, whom you love, go to the land of Moriah, and offer him there as a burnt offering on one of the mountains I will tell you about." Then Abraham said to his young men, "Stay here with the donkey. The boy and I will go over there to worship; then we'll come back to you." (Gen. 22:2, 5)*

Have you ever sensed God's presence in some situation in your life—beyond your normal assurance that God is always there? Was worshipping God part of that encounter? Abraham and Isaac experienced God in worship in that private and intimate moment on the mountain, and it changed all of our lives forever—because Abraham's faith in action set the example for every generation to come. And God responded!

Just as God was present with Abraham on that day, so also God will be present when we worship—whether we're alone or gathered with other believers to express our worship. God has promised, and He is always faithful.

Something Special Happens When We Worship Together

Though God is always present whenever and wherever we worship, I know from personal experience that something very special can happen when we come together to worship corporately—particularly when a stadium full of men gathers to worship! A few years ago, I joined fifteen men from our church at a Promise Keepers event in Texas Stadium. Honestly, I didn't want to go. I had so many details pressing in with my role as music minister at our church; but I had made a commitment to the guys, and so I went. I didn't know it at the time, but I had an appointment with God Almighty that day.

We were late to the stadium and ended up in the end zone about as far from the platform as you can get. But it really didn't matter. God was there. He was all over the stadium. As the hearts and voices of more than sixty thousand men rose toward heaven that day, our God responded—He truly inhabited the praises of His people.

That day the speaker's message really didn't make a difference for me. The only thing that mattered was God's amazing presence in the midst of our uninhibited worship. As the speaker proclaimed God's call for ministers to move forward in their calling, those precious brothers laid hands on me and prayed me "forward in ministry" right there on the Astroturf at Texas Stadium. Roger Staubach had thrown touchdowns for the Cowboys in that very end zone, but God scored a life-changing touchdown in my heart that day!

I could never describe the overwhelming power of God's presence that day as I knelt and wept my way to the very throne of God. He was there! God always inhabits the praises of His people.

Call to Worship

The trumpeters and singers joined together to praise and thank the LORD with one voice. They raised their voices, accompanied by trumpets, cymbals, and musical instruments, in praise to the LORD:
For He is good;
His faithful love endures forever;
the temple, the LORD's temple, was filled with a cloud. And because of the cloud, the priests were not able to continue ministering, for the glory of the LORD filled God's temple. (2 Chron. 5:13–14)

Can you imagine being part of a worship service like that? The singers and musicians, priests, and other leaders surely prepared for this moment for months, if not years. Certainly there was an "order of worship" that day, just like most of us have in our church services. But God had something in mind that wasn't in the bulletin!

God truly delights in the praises of His people, then and now. Why not join the worship in heaven right now and shout: For the Lord *is* good! His mercy endures forever!

Reflections

- We were made to worship God, and as we worship, we make a "dwelling place" or place of habitation for God.
- Worship occurs both privately (individually) and corporately, and God inhabits both kinds of worship.
- As we spend time in God's presence, He directs us and empowers us to respond.
- God always inhabits the praises of His people.

Prayer

*Dear Savior, thank You for the promise of Your presence!
Lord, let my motivation to serve You grow out of my
time in Your presence! Empower me as I bow before
Your Lordship in my life. Amen.*

5

Seven Words of Worship

*Learning to experience God in worship is a process that
can be aided by seven simple words.*

Every good contractor knows that the foundation is crucial if a build-ing is going to stand the test of time and fulfill the vision of the architect who designed it. A good foundation in worship is reinforced by these foundational truths:

- God really does want a real, personal relationship with us.
- In light of who God is and all He has done, our response must be worship.
- As we worship, God has promised to be present.
- Worship is the key to a lifetime of experiencing God!

God has promised to meet us as we worship, and we are completely worthy of His holy presence because of His great sacrifice in Jesus Christ. This is what worship really is: our response to God's revelation of who He is and what He has done. As we respond, He really will be present. Then we truly experience God in worship!

Building on the Foundation Together

The foundation is set, and now it's time to start the building. It's time to build together our understanding of worship so that we can experience complete freedom to honor God more fully with our hearts, our individual voices, and our everyday lives.

The apostle Paul wrote:

> *For we are God's co-workers. You are God's field, God's building. According to God's grace that was given to me, as a skilled master builder I have laid a foundation, and another builds on it. But each one must be careful how he builds on it, because no one can lay any other foundation than what has been laid—that is, Jesus Christ. (1 Cor. 3:9–11)*

Jesus Christ is our focus. He is the One who is worthy of our worship, and He is the One we will worship throughout all of eternity. Jesus is the reason we worship; He is the recipient of our worship and the One who responds to our sacrifice of praise. Jesus is the cornerstone of everything. Now it's time to build!

Seven Simple Words

As we learn to experience God in worship, we need a good blueprint to follow. Even the most talented builders are only as good as the blueprints in front of them. Our building process will be guided by seven simple words and the biblically based summary statement that follows them. You have heard these words before, but perhaps not in the worship context: **creation, grace, love, response, expression, presence,** and **experience**.

> *Each of us was **created** by God for relationship with Him, but we can only enjoy that relationship by God's **grace**. God's great **love** for us, demonstrated in Christ Jesus, initiates our **response**. The only reasonable and adequate response is our **expression** of worship. As we worship, God has promised His **presence**. We can always **experience** God in worship!*

These seven words of worship can become your keys to a lifetime of experiencing God. We were made to worship Him in every part of our lives. Because of His great sacrifice in Christ Jesus, we are free to come boldly before the throne of God and expect a loving encounter with our God and King. The Cornerstone is in place.

Call to Worship

Let's take a brief look at each of these seven words of worship and the definition that follows:

Creation—anything caused to come into existence; made, originated

Grace—goodwill or favor

Love—a strong, passionate affection for someone or something

Response—something said or done in answer or reply

Expression—putting into words, stating

Presence—the fact or state of being at a specified place

Experience—the act of living through an event, anything and everything observed or lived through training and personal participation

Reflections

- God made us for relationship, and He is the initiator of this relationship; all we have to do is respond.
- Worship is our response to God's revelation of who He is and what He has done.
- Worship is vitally important to our lives.
- God has promised to meet us as we worship.
- Seven words of worship can become our guide to experiencing God throughout a lifetime of worship.
- We are worthy of God's holy presence because of His great sacrifice in Jesus Christ.
- We can always experience God in worship!

Prayer

God, thank You for inviting me into Your presence! Give me a growing hunger to know You and desire Your presence in my life. Thank You for being my High Priest and making a way for me to enter into Your presence! Amen.

CREATION

Song of Worship

"We Were Made to Worship"

You and I were made to worship Him.
We were made to bow before His throne.
He delights when we lift our voice in praise to Him.
We were made to worship Christ alone.
Holy, holy, holy is our King.
Worthy, worthy, to Him our praise we bring.

WORDS AND MUSIC BY TERRY MACALMON
COPYRIGHT 2006 TMMI MUSIC (ADMIN. BY MUSIC SERVICES) ASCAP

6

Created for Relationship

Each of us was **created** by God for
relationship with Him.

*God created us in His image so that we might have a
relationship with Him and fulfill His purpose on the earth.*

*In the beginning was the Word, and the Word was with God,
and the Word was God. He was with God in the beginning.
All things were created through Him, and apart from Him not
one thing was created that has been created. (John 1:1–3)*

The Bible is clear: God has always been the initiator of relationship,
and we are designed and equipped to respond. God created heaven
and earth. He created man and woman and provided for their needs—
including a place to meet with God Himself. In fact, the entire order
and depth of God's creation indicates that we were created in God's
image so that we might have a relationship with Him and fulfill His
purpose on the earth.

Created in His Image

The story unfolds in the first chapter of Genesis. God *spoke,* and amazing things happened.

God *spoke* light and entire solar systems into existence:

> Then God said, "Let there be light," and there was light. (Gen. 1:3)
>
> Then God said, "Let there be lights in the expanse of the sky to separate the day from the night. They will serve as signs for festivals and for days and years. They will be lights in the expanse of the sky to provide light on the earth." And it was so. (Gen. 1:14–15)

God *spoke* water and land into existence and created every living thing—every plant and every animal that has ever lived on the face of the earth:

> Then God said, "Let the water under the sky be gathered into one place, and let the dry land appear." And it was so. God called the dry land "earth," and He called the gathering of the water "seas." And God saw that it was good. (Gen. 1:9–10)
>
> Then God said, "Let the earth produce vegetation: seed-bearing plants, and fruit trees on the earth bearing fruit with seed in it, according to their kinds." And it was so. (Gen. 1:11)
>
> Then God said, "Let the water swarm with living creatures, and let birds fly above the earth across the expanse of the sky." . . . So God made the wildlife of the earth according to their kinds, the livestock according to their kinds, and creatures that crawl on the ground according to their kinds. And God saw that it was good. (Gen. 1:20, 25)

But when it came to creating man, God reached down from heaven as a master craftsman at work, shaping the masterpiece—the centerpiece—of His creation. Yes, God created something unique when He formed man from the dust of the earth—something above and beyond, quite different from all other created things.

The Genesis story is clear:

Then the LORD God formed the man out of the dust from the ground and breathed the breath of life into his nostrils, and the man became a living being. (Gen. 2:7)

Then God said, "Let Us make man in Our image, according to Our likeness." (Gen. 1:26)

For God made man in His image. (Gen. 9:6)

And the rest of the biblical story, from Genesis to Revelation, affirms that we are the embodiment of the image of God. He fully equipped us with His attributes. God gave us intellect and the ability to reason. He made us with a will and emotions. Unlike every other part of God's creation, God fashioned us in His own image. We have been given exactly what we need to fulfill His purpose for our lives.

Created for His Purpose

After creating man and woman, God bestowed His blessing on them and empowered them with a mission—a purpose:

So God created man in His own image; He created him in the image of God; He created them male and female.
God blessed them, and God said to them, "Be fruitful, multiply; fill the earth, and subdue it. Rule the fish of the sea, the birds of the sky, and every creature that crawls on the earth." (Gen. 1:27–28)

God told Adam and Eve to populate the earth and exercise dominion over every other created thing. God revealed Himself and His plans for Adam and Eve, just as He continues to reveal Himself and His desire for us today. Our role is to respond to His revelation with worship as we fulfill our purpose, both individually and corporately.

For we are His creation—created in Christ Jesus for good works, which God prepared ahead of time so that we should walk in them. (Eph. 2:10)

From the first lines of the Genesis story throughout the pages of the Bible, God communicates His desire for us to know who He is, who we are in relationship to Him, how we should respond, and what we can expect. God created us in His image, and He has chosen to work through us to tend to His creation and fulfill His will on the earth—to do the good works He has prepared or planned for us. God wants to reveal Himself and His will to us every day, and as we respond we can experience God as He works through us.

The Bible makes clear that each individual is God's creation, and that He created us with His purpose in mind. Just like Adam and Eve, God created us to fulfill His purpose!

1. *Purpose* precedes creation.

Creation occurs in the mind and heart of the creator. The creator conceptualizes the reason for creating something before the creation ever exists. For example, when building a house, the architect (creator) must begin with the purpose for the structure before the design can be formalized. God knew exactly what He had in mind before He created you and me.

> For it was You who created my inward parts;
> You knit me together in my mother's womb.
> I will praise You,
> because I have been remarkably and wonderfully made.
> Your works are wonderful,
> and I know this very well.
> My bones were not hidden from You
> when I was made in secret,
> when I was formed in the depths of the earth.
> Your eyes saw me when I was formless;
> all my days were written in Your book and planned
> before a single one of them began. (Ps. 139:13–16)

2. *Purpose* determines design.

Once the purpose is determined, a design is developed to accomplish that purpose. For example, the inventor (creator) of the fork and spoon clearly determined the purpose of each instrument before developing the design. The spoon was needed to transport liquids, and its shape dictated that purpose. Likewise, God determined our design *before* He created us!

> For we are His creation—created in Christ Jesus for good works, which God prepared ahead of time so that we should walk in them. (Eph. 2:10)

3. Our *purpose* coincides with our gifts and abilities.

God created ducks to float on water and fly through the air. He gave them the characteristics of buoyancy and flight. In the same way, God has given us gifts and abilities that coincide with His plans for humanity.

We are the body of Christ, and God fulfills His purposes on the earth through us. We were made in God's image with the ability to create, reason, and communicate unlike any other living creation He made. And each of us has been given specific talents, gifts, and abilities to fulfill His purposes. Our design is not an accident!

> Now as we have many parts in one body, and all the parts do not have the same function, in the same way we who are many are one body in Christ and individually members of one another. According to the grace given to us, we have different gifts: If prophecy, use it according to the standard of faith; if service, in service; if teaching, in teaching; if exhorting, in exhortation; giving, with generosity; leading, with diligence; showing mercy, with cheerfulness. (Rom. 12:4–8)

4. Our *purpose* is defined in our nature.

Have you noticed that we are often drawn to something or some activity in a seemingly natural way? That's also the way it is in our relationship with God. Because God made us for relationship, we have been given the ability and desire to relate to God. We are the way we are because of *why* we are!

> As a deer longs for streams of water,
> so I long for You, God.
> I thirst for God, the living God.
> When can I come and appear before God? (Ps. 42:1–2)

5. Our *purpose* requires a disciplined response.

Our *overall purpose* is clearly defined in Genesis 1:28: to populate the earth and exercise dominion over it. However, our *unique purpose* can be found only as we develop our relationship with God. Growing that relationship requires daily attention through prayer, study of God's Word, and worship. And that is where we find our unique individual purpose—in God's presence.

*Until I come, give your attention to public reading,
exhortation, and teaching. Do not neglect the gift that is in
you; it was given to you through prophecy, with the laying
on of hands by the council of elders. Practice these things;
be committed to them, so that your progress may be evident
to all. Be conscientious about yourself and your teaching;
persevere in these things, for by doing this you will save both
yourself and your hearers. (1 Tim. 4:13–16)*

Call to Worship

God desires a loving, personal relationship with us. He is continually searching for people who will respond to who He is and all He has done. God created us in His image, for His purpose, and for His presence. Our only reasonable and adequate response is worship (see Rom. 12:1).

Reflections

- All things were made by God—for Him and through Him. That includes us!
- God created us with great purpose in mind.
- Purpose precedes creation, determines design, is defined in our nature, coincides with our gifts and abilities, and requires a disciplined response.

Prayer

*Heavenly Father, thank You for creating me with purpose and
for a purpose! Help me to see how Your design of my life has
given me a unique place in Your kingdom. Amen.*

7

Created for His Presence

God inhabits the praises of His people—
He will always meet us there.

As we have seen, God created us in His image to fulfill His purpose—
His will. But God also created us simply to enjoy His presence.

God's desire for relationship with man was evident from the beginning. God chose to speak many things into existence, but He chose to *speak to* man—and an eternal relationship was formed. God even provided a special place for Adam and Eve, a place where God Himself would come and meet with them. We read about this special place in Genesis 2 and 3:

> The LORD God planted a garden in Eden, in the east, and there He placed the man He had formed. (Gen. 2:8)
>
> The LORD God took the man and placed him in the garden of Eden to work it and watch over it. (Gen. 2:15)
>
> Then the man and his wife heard the sound of the LORD God walking in the garden at the time of the evening breeze. (Gen. 3:8)

When God placed Adam and Eve in the garden, the stage was set. Can you imagine what that must have been like? The atmosphere, the land, the air, the food, and the animals—the whole earth was made for them, and they were made for it. All the efforts of the Creator were made for their benefit, and the One who made such a marvelous place for them to live actually chose to dwell there with them.

God's desire was to provide a wonderful place for Adam and Eve. He loved them unconditionally and wanted to be with them and meet all their needs—just as He desires to be with us and meet our needs today.

Those of us who are parents want the same for our children. My wife, Teresa, and I didn't have resources as vast as God's, to be sure, but I still remember our efforts to create just the right place for our first son, Lee.

Our home at that time looked like any other tiny two-bedroom apartment in Baton Rouge, Louisiana, but to us, it really was a gift from God. It was also a gift from a very generous man who attended the church where I served as associate music and youth minister who charged us half what he could have rented the apartment for to anyone else. I was in my last year of seminary in New Orleans—a two-hour drive down the interstate—and as you can imagine, there wasn't a lot left in our bank account at the end of the month.

It was such an exciting time. We both knew that God had called us to ministry and had provided a wonderful church to fulfill that call on our lives. Even as a young couple, Teresa and I had a clear sense of God's purpose for our lives: serving the local church.

It was September. I was only three days away from the final oral exam that would earn my master's degree in church music, and I was about to become a father for the very first time! I hoped and prayed those two events wouldn't happen on the same day. And God answered my prayer—but just barely!

Three days before my final exam, I became a dad. I can't begin to describe how excited I was (and still am) to have a wonderful son like Lee. My professors were gracious. The first question in my exam was, "Tell us about that son of yours!" I talked as long as they would let me. Then the real questions started to fly. By the grace of God, I passed. I had a diploma for my wall and a baby for the spare bedroom!

Teresa and I didn't have much money, but we had family and friends. Together we had turned that spare bedroom into a pretty special place for young Lee. And on the day he came home from the hospital, he was surrounded by expressions of love from friends, neighbors, grandparents, and, of course, Mom and Dad.

That little apartment that had been God's gift to Teresa and me was a perfect fit for all three of us. God had provided exactly what we needed to fulfill our role as new parents, just as He had provided everything we needed to fulfill our purpose in ministry. As our family has grown so have the places we have lived. God has always given us what we needed to have a home. And just as with Adam and Eve in the garden of Eden, He chose to dwell there with us.

Created for Worship

Adam and Eve were given everything by God, including the privilege of dwelling in His glorious presence. They had every reason to understand who God was and all He had done for them, but they turned their affections away from God and toward their own desires. They had firsthand revelation of who God was and what He had done for them—they were created to worship and serve God—yet they chose to listen to the adversary instead. Their improper response to God's revelation made His presence a frightening experience.

> Then the man and his wife heard the sound of the LORD God walking in the garden at the time of the evening breeze, and they hid themselves from the LORD God among the trees of the garden. (Gen. 3:8)

Just as God was searching the garden for Adam on that day, so also He has searched throughout all of time for those who would respond to His gracious gift of life, worship Him, and remain in His glorious presence. Worship is the place of meeting—the place of enthronement for God—and He will always meet us there.

Adam and Eve made a decision that set the course of human history in the wrong direction. They chose to respond to Satan's lie rather than to what they knew of God and all He had done for them. In one simple act of disobedience, they showed more reverence for Satan's words of doubt than for God's loving revelation and provision for them.

Adam and Eve were created for worship, and so are we. The need and propensity to worship was inside them, just as it is inside us. The actual definition of the word *worship* is to show religious reverence and intense love or admiration for a deity.[1] We were created to respond to God's revelation with worship, which is our show of "religious reverence and intense love and admiration" for God and God alone.

Whether it happens at a concert, a sporting event, a Broadway play, a corporate boardroom, or a Las Vegas showroom, people continually gather to worship someone or something. The deep need to respond to someone or something with our expression of appreciation and adoration is simply part of our DNA as human beings. We were created for worship.

Call to Worship

It really isn't hard to believe that we were created to worship something or someone, is it? The real question is *what* or *whom are we worshipping?* It's a matter of where we center our focus. We can always identify what is "first and foremost" in our lives by taking a hard look at what attracts our attention the most.

As the Bible tells us, God is jealous of our time and our attention, and He deserves first place in our lives. As we grow in revelation of who He is and what He alone has done in our lives, we really will experience God in worship. Our journey has just begun.

Reflections

- Adam and Eve had firsthand revelation of who God is and what He had done for them, yet they chose to listen to the adversary instead of worshipping God.
- People are made for worship, and we are going to worship something or someone.
- Worship takes many outward forms—whether we are worshipping God or something/someone else.

Prayer

Lord, I praise You for making me in Your image. Let my life bring glory to You and to Your name! Give me the wisdom to see when I am giving my worship to anything or anyone else. I want to worship You alone. Amen.

Notes

1. *Webster's New World Dictionary*, Pocket Books Paperback Edition, © 2003 Wiley Publishing, Inc.

8

Faith-filled Worship

Worship requires faith, and God always responds
to faith-filled worship.

Revelation is crucial to worship. True revelation comes only from God (see Matt. 16:16–17), and faith is essential. There is perhaps no better example of faith than Abraham. He certainly failed from time to time as the rest of us do, but his faith in God consistently produced obedience—and he was continually rewarded. His story begins in Genesis 12 with a journey to an unknown place that God would later reveal.

Abraham Steps Out in Faith

As we first meet Abraham, his name is actually Abram:

> *The LORD said to Abram:*
> *Go out from your land,*
> *your relatives,*
> *and your father's house*
> *to the land that I will show you.*

I will make you into a great nation,
I will bless you,
I will make your name great,
and you will be a blessing.
I will bless those who bless you,
I will curse those who treat you with contempt,
and all the peoples on earth
will be blessed through you.
So Abram went, as the LORD *had told him, and Lot went with*
him. Abram was 75 years old when he left Haran.
(Gen. 12:1–4)

Abram took his family and his possessions and left Haran, a prominent trading center, and headed for unfamiliar and dangerous territory. Can you imagine such a decision? He must have known there would be severe challenges ahead. Surely he assumed there were plenty of tribes and nations occupying the land that God promised to give to him, and they weren't going to leave voluntarily.

To make matters worse, once he got to Canaan, the land of promise, there was a severe famine. In fact, it was so severe that Abram fled to Egypt where he tried to pass his wife off as his sister in order to save his own hide.

There was a famine in the land, so Abram went down to
Egypt to live there for a while because the famine in the land
was severe. When he was about to enter Egypt, he said to
his wife Sarai, "Look, I know what a beautiful woman you are.
When the Egyptians see you, they will say, 'This is his wife.'
They will kill me but let you live. Please say you're my sister
so it will go well for me because of you, and my life will be
spared on your account." (Gen. 12:10–13)

Ultimately Abram returned to Canaan, parted company with his nephew Lot, and turned his attention to making the best of what looked like the least part of the land of promise:

Now Lot, who was traveling with Abram, also had flocks,
herds, and tents. But the land was unable to support them as
long as they stayed together, for they had so many posses-
sions that they could not stay together, and there was quar-
reling between the herdsmen of Abram's livestock and the

herdsmen of Lot's livestock. At that time the Canaanites and the Perizzites were living in the land.

Then Abram said to Lot, "Please, let's not have quarreling between you and me, or between your herdsmen and my herdsmen, since we are relatives. Isn't the whole land before you? Separate from me: if you go to the left, I will go to the right; if you go to the right, I will go to the left." (Gen. 13:5–9)

Abram continued to step out in faith as he rescued Lot and Lot's family from certain death in Sodom. His exploits are recorded in Genesis 14. But one thing was missing: Abram had no direct descendant to fulfill God's promise to make him a great nation.

Yet God had a plan and a promise for Abram that was almost impossible for him to believe:

After these events, the word of the LORD came to Abram in a vision:

Do not be afraid, Abram. I am your shield; your reward will be very great.

But Abram said, "Lord GOD, what can You give me, since I am childless and the heir of my house is Eliezer of Damascus?" Abram continued, "Look, You have given me no offspring, so a slave born in my house will be my heir."

Now the word of the LORD came to him: "This one will not be your heir; instead, one who comes from your own body will be your heir." He took him outside and said, "Look at the sky and count the stars, if you are able to count them." Then He said to him, "Your offspring will be that numerous."

Abram believed the LORD, and He credited it to him as righteousness. (Gen. 15:1–6)

God made an everlasting covenant with Abram, and ultimately Abram became Abraham, the father of many nations and the father of our faith. Yet there was another test of faith that Abraham had to face—perhaps the ultimate test of his faith. Abraham had experienced a lifetime of relationship with God—a lifetime of revelation of who God is and what God had done; and that revelation was about to lead to the ultimate act of worship in the midst of the major test of Abraham's life.

Abraham's Ultimate Test of Faith

The first mention of the word *worship* in the Bible is found in Genesis 22. In this chapter, Abraham was facing the ultimate test of his dedication and obedience to God. He was about to climb the mountain to sacrifice his son, Isaac, as God had instructed him:

> *"Take your son," He said, "your only son Isaac, whom you love, go to the land of Moriah, and offer him there as a burnt offering on one of the mountains I will tell you about."*
> *(Gen. 22:2)*

Abraham was ready to obey God before he knew what would happen. He was about to experience God in worship—faith-filled worship!

Why would Abraham be so willing to obey God? Because God had proven His commitment to Abraham in the fulfillment of His promise. Abraham knew he could trust God.

When I was ten years old, my dad proved himself to me in a way I've never forgotten. He was the manager of a big grocery store that was part of a well-known chain of big stores. He had a district boss, Mr. Johnson, whom our family knew all about. Mom used to say she could tell when Mr. Johnson was coming to town because Dad would be grouchy for the few days leading up to the inspection. One summer day I was hanging out at the store as I often did when school was out, doing odd jobs for my dad. Unexpectedly Mr. Johnson walked in for an inspection. He was a big man with a booming voice and salty language. I felt a little intimidated by him, to say the least. Mr. Johnson seemed to be in a good mood this particular day and, with me standing right there by my dad, began to tell a story with his usual colorful language. Most dads would have fumbled for a quarter and sent the son off for a snack but not my dad! He interrupted Mr. Johnson and said, "Sir, this is my son Mike. I don't use language like that and I would appreciate it if you wouldn't either around my son." A little startled, Mr. Johnson stopped his story, sort of apologized and moved on to the business he had come to conduct with my dad. I felt ten feet tall and thought my dad was twenty feet tall! He had proven that he valued me more than his job or his relationship with his boss. Moments like that made it easy for me throughout my life to want to please my dad—whatever he asked me to do.

That kind of trust is why Abraham, when he heard God's voice, could follow His direction unreservedly.

> Then Abraham said to his young men, "Stay here with the donkey. The boy and I will go over there to worship; then we'll come back to you." (Gen. 22:5)

Abraham knew what he was about to do—he was going to sacrifice the child of promise. Can you imagine what it must have required for Abraham to have the faith to obey God? His sacrifice would be an act of worship, and he believed *by faith* that God would meet them at their point of faithfulness and need. What's more, he expected Isaac to worship God as well.

In the natural, Abraham's act of worship could cost him everything—his hope, his future, his promise from God Himself. Surely Abraham experienced a crisis of belief! Surely he had his doubts. But Abraham knew *by faith* that he and Isaac would be back. He had had a revelation of God, and he knew His God would not let him down! Abraham's worship—his act of obedience—was in direct response to that revelation.

The Hebrew word for *worship* used in Genesis 22:5 is the word *shachah*. It is used more than one hundred times in the Old Testament, and it provides a picture of someone bowing, kneeling, stooping, or prostrating on the ground before God—the one who is *lesser* responding to the One who is clearly *greater*. The use of this word always indicated a physical action that was required of God's people.

The Jewish people were consistent in the outward expression of worship, but the word *shachah* also has a great deal to do with the condition of the heart of the worshipper. Abraham's act of worship made it clear: God's acceptance of our worship continues to be totally dependent on our belief—our faith—that He is our only source, and that apart from Him we can do nothing. As Jesus said,

> "I am the vine; you are the branches. The one who remains in Me and I in him produces much fruit, because you can do nothing without Me. If anyone does not remain in Me, he is thrown aside like a branch and he withers. They gather them, throw them into the fire, and they are burned. If you remain in Me and My words remain in you, ask whatever you want and it will be done for you. My Father is glorified by this: that you produce much fruit and prove to be My disciples." (John 15:5–8)

Worship Is Costly . . . But the Reward Is Great!

Worship is not always easy and often costs the worshipper a great deal, yet the reward is great: we bear much fruit, prove to be Jesus' disciples, and glorify our Father. At the very least, the "cost" of worship includes our time and attention. We all encounter the pressing issues of life daily, yet it is possible to abide—to live, remain, and dwell—in Christ.

Abraham is a wonderful example to us all. As we've noted previously, he spent a great deal of time in God's presence. As a result, he believed God's promises. When the time came to act on his faith, Abraham responded with faith—the same faith that is available to us today as we spend time in God's presence, receiving and believing His Word. When we see God for who He is, our hearts are forever changed—and we respond with worship. And God always responds to faith-filled worship. He wants us to set aside time to simply enjoy His presence and listen for His direction in our lives.

Take a look at the following verses:

> *"Take your son," He said, "your only son Isaac, whom you love, go to the land of Moriah, and offer him there as a burnt offering on one of the mountains I will tell you about."*
> *So early in the morning Abraham got up, saddled his donkey, and took with him two of his young men and his son Isaac. He split wood for a burnt offering and set out to go to the place God had told him about. (Gen. 22:2–3)*

Once Abraham received revelation of God's desire for Isaac's sacrifice, how long did it take him to respond? Apparently, he heard from God and stepped out in faith the very next day! If God revealed something that would require your *ultimate* act of worship and sacrifice, how long do you think it might take you to respond?

Call to Worship

Abraham is a great example of a man who chose to act on God's invitation to join Him as He worked. God revealed Himself and His purpose to Abraham, yet just like you and me, Abraham still had to respond. Although Abraham surely must have had a crisis of belief as God revealed His plan for Abraham's life, his response was *worship*.

Abraham went through the same process that we all face today as we respond to God's purposes in our lives. He is the Bible's ultimate example of a man who chose to "stay the course" and believe God in the midst of the most challenging circumstances. Abraham *knew* God, and he responded in the moment of ultimate crisis with *worship*—and so must we.

Reflections

- The first use of the word *worship* in the Bible is found in Genesis 22:5 as Abraham prepared to sacrifice Isaac.
- *Shachah* is the Hebrew word for *worship* meaning to bow, kneel, or stoop before God.
- Worship requires faith.
- God is only interested in faith-filled, heartfelt worship, and God *always* responds to this kind of worship.
- Worship is not always easy and often costs the worshipper a great deal.
- Abraham's encounter with God as He prepared to sacrifice Isaac is a great example of experiencing God in worship.

Prayer

Father, thank You for the example of Abraham. Would You open my eyes to those sacrifices You would ask of me in worship? Would You give me the faith to trust You even when I don't understand? Amen.

9

Revelation Is Essential for Worship

Spending time with God to gain revelation is essential for worship.

The story of Abraham and Isaac in Genesis 22 gives us a firsthand look at worship in response to God's revelation. Abraham had a lifetime of interaction with God, and he had seen God's intervention in his life repeatedly. When it came time for the "ultimate act of worship," Abraham was ready to respond. Abraham had a clear revelation of God; he knew who was the *greater* and who was the *lesser* in the relationship because he had spent a great deal of time in God's presence.

Abraham had a correct view of God, and so must we as we worship.

Having a Correct View of God

When God gave the Ten Commandments to Moses on Mount Sinai, He made a statement about His requirement for worship. Number one on God's list was a clear understanding of His position as the one and only true God:

*"Do not have other gods besides Me. Do not make an idol
for yourself, whether in the shape of anything in the heavens
above or on the earth below or in the waters under the earth.
You must not bow down to them or worship them."
(Exod. 20:3–5)*

By His grace and mercy, God had delivered His people from
Egyptian slavery. They hadn't earned that deliverance; He had chosen
them. God had called them to Himself, and now He was telling them
how they were to live within the freedom He had given them. They
were created for God's purpose—to worship Him and dwell in His
presence forever—and so are we.

However, God was dealing with an ungrateful people who consistently complained about His intervention in their lives. God's response
was to write the Ten Commandments on stone tablets so there would
be no doubt about His instructions for them. Just before God burned
the Ten Commandments into stone, He made this proclamation:

*"I am the LORD your God, who brought you out of the land of
Egypt, out of the place of slavery." (Exod. 20:2)*

God wanted to remind His people who He was and who they were to
worship.

Having a correct view of God is essential to worship. Without a
clear understanding of God's awesome nature and supernatural power
in relationship to our own human failings and limitations, we simply
can't worship with our whole hearts. We must understand that we desperately need God, and that He is willing and able to intervene in our
lives here and now.

Although God had proven His faithfulness and care for the Israelites
over and over again, they simply didn't get it. God had to make the
statement "I am the LORD your God," many times throughout the days
of the Old Testament because His people were continually distracted by
other things, which would become the gods they worshipped.

We still need to be reminded today that God is "the Lord our
God" because we, too, face so many distractions. The allure of other
gods is all around us. Every form of communication and entertainment
is calling us to worship something or someone other than the true King
of kings.

Spending Time in God's Presence

I will never forget the first time I ever saw my wife Teresa. It was a Sunday night service at Calvary Baptist Church in Cleveland, Mississippi, where I was the part-time minister of music. The incoming freshmen at Delta State University had moved into the dorms that day and Teresa, being the faithful pastor's daughter that she is, wanted to start off her college career right by going to church that night. She was late getting there, and she walked through the back door during the first hymn. As I spotted her and a few friends making their way to their seats, I thought, "Now there's a follow-up visit to a prospect I'd like to make!" Needless to say, I was struck by her beauty immediately. I didn't meet her that night, but the next day I saw her in the music building and learned she was a music major! "Things are looking good," I thought! Then, later in the week, I saw her at a Baptist Student event and finally had the courage to meet her. I didn't ask her out then, but I sure wanted to.

A couple of weeks later, I saw her crossing the campus and decided it was time to take the plunge. I asked her if she was going to be in town that weekend, to which she replied, "I don't think so. I may be going home. Why do you ask?" (Later she told me that she thought I was going to ask her to sing at my church and that she really didn't want to, so she made up her reason why she wouldn't be on campus that weekend.) Then I told her, "I wanted to ask you to go to the football game with me on Saturday." She immediately changed her story. "Oh, I'll be here and I would love to!" It was the beginning of the relationship with the love of my life. From that day on, no one ever had to make me spend time with Teresa. I loved every minute of our time together. (I still do!) As a matter of fact, we spent almost every evening together "studying" the week before our first official date. Hey, I was really studying. I was studying *her*! Whenever we sang together, I knew she was the girl for me!

In the same way, as we grow in our love for God, we will spend time getting to know Him. And as we spend time with Him, our love for Him will grow. Our worship must always be in response to *God's* revelation, and the only way to understand who God is and what He has done is to spend time in His presence. We must be intentional about spending time with God and keeping our focus on Him. Unless we position ourselves to hear from God, there can be no revelation. And without revelation, our worship will be hindered.

As we have seen, Abraham worshipped *by faith* in response to God's revelation when he prepared to offer his son, Isaac, as a sacrifice. In the book of Hebrews, we read about Abraham's faith:

> By faith Abraham, when he was tested, offered up Isaac; he who had received the promises was offering up his unique son, about whom it had been said, "In Isaac your seed will be called." He considered God to be able even to raise someone from the dead, from which he also got him back as an illustration. (Heb. 11:17–19)

Abraham developed that kind of faith by spending time in God's presence. He had a clear revelation of who God was and what God had done in his life. He *believed* that God was able to raise Isaac from the dead, and he knew God would respond to his expression of worship. Abraham was a very successful man with a large family and many possessions, yet he didn't allow the pressures or encumbrances of life to interfere with his personal relationship with God.

Webster's International Dictionary defines *encumbrance* as "someone or something that hinders or burdens an individual."[2] Encumbrances, or hindrances, also include things and activities that distract us from our focus on God. Encumbrances restrict us from the abundant life that Jesus promised in John 10:10.

We all face a litany of distractions in our lives. Even good things can be a distraction from time spent with God. Television, movies, books, music, sports, debts, maintenance of possessions, career obsession, material gain, competition . . . shall I go on?

> Therefore since we also have such a large cloud of witnesses surrounding us, let us lay aside every weight and the sin that so easily ensnares us, and run with endurance the race that lies before us. (Heb. 12:1)

A Call to Worship

Spending time with God on a regular and continuing basis requires intentional action on our part. The process of life is filled with responsibilities, and many are good and necessary. However, no good or necessary part of life can replace the deep need we have to spend time in the presence of God Almighty.

> I have asked one thing from the LORD;
> it is what I desire:

to dwell in the house of the LORD
all the days of my life,
gazing on the beauty of the LORD
and seeking Him in His temple. (Ps. 27:4)

It is in God's presence that we really come to know Him—and ourselves. God makes many great and precious promises to His children throughout Scripture, and their value to our lives is based on our ability to believe and receive all He has promised. But how can we believe One we do not know? It's simply not possible!

Spending time in God's presence—getting to know Him in the most intimate parts of our heart and soul—gives us the foundation to really believe all He has planned for those of us who love Him and are called according to His purposes. There is no substitute for time spent in God's presence.

Reflections

- God's number one requirement for worship is that we have a clear understanding, or a correct view, of who He is: He is the Lord our God.
- The allure of other gods is all around us; we face many distractions that threaten to shift our focus and our worship from God to something or someone else.
- Abraham had plenty of reasons to be distracted or hindered in his time with God, but he overcame these hindrances and heard God clearly. We can too.
- We must make a commitment of time in order to gain revelation; time spent with the Lord is time well spent.

Prayer

Dear Lord, give me to strength to remove those things in my life that take the place of my time with You. Help me prioritize my day so that You have first place. Lord, help me make my calendar reflect my desire to know You. Amen.

10

A Place to Worship

God is in us and among us, and His presence
is available every time we worship Him.

On the heels of giving the Israelites the Ten Commandments, God instructed the people to build a place for worship—a place where He would dwell. This place, the tabernacle, became the place where God would establish His residence on the earth—a place where God's people could worship freely and spend time in His presence.

The Tabernacle: God's Dwelling Place

The tabernacle was a rare and holy place. It was where God chose to dwell. It was where God met with His people and received their sacrifices. The tabernacle was the place God chose to live on earth:

> *"I will dwell among the Israelites and be their God."*
> (Exod. 29:45).

The tabernacle—and later the temple—would be the place where God would relate corporately to His people in worship. This was the place that was set apart for God and His people.

King David is regarded as a great warrior and king. But perhaps he is best known for his role as a worshipper and worship leader. God continually revealed Himself to David—in both the good times and the difficult times—and David's response was worship.

Meeting with God was crucial to King David throughout his reign. In fact, once he was established as king in Jerusalem, his first action was to prepare a place for the ark of God, the resident place of God's presence, power, and Word:

> David built houses for himself in the city of David, and he prepared a place for the ark of God and pitched a tent for it. Then David said, "No one but the Levites may carry the ark of God, because the LORD has chosen them to carry the ark of the LORD and to minister before Him forever."
> David assembled all Israel at Jerusalem to bring the ark of the LORD to the place he had prepared for it.
> (1 Chron. 15:1–3)

King David knew God's people needed to encounter God's presence just as he had done his whole life. Their lives depended upon their relationship with God. There could be no true worship without a relationship between the One being worshipped and the worshipper. That was true in the Old Testament, and it is still true today.

Everything changed, however, when God provided Jesus Christ—the Lamb who was slain for all our sin and iniquity. Our relationship with God was sealed forever by the blood of the Lamb.

Our Hearts: God's New Dwelling Place

Sometimes for fun I'll ask people to guess who would be the most famous person I have ever sung with in a duet. I enjoy the shock on their faces when I give the answer. Hands down, no contest, the most famous person I've ever sung with is basketball legend Pistol Pete Maravich. Here's the story:

I was living in Baton Rouge when my good friend and LSU swim coach Rick Meador asked me to sing for a Fellowship of Christian Athletes program at the university. Then he told me Pistol Pete was going to be the speaker. Wow! I couldn't believe it! Being the sports fan that I am, I was excited to be on the program with the man many consider to be the greatest basketball player of all time.

When the night came, I met Rick and Pete for dinner. After we ate, Pete and I went to the meeting hall for a sound check. He asked me if I knew the Imperials song "Oh Buddah," and I told him I did. He explained that was his favorite song because he had tried many of the religions the song talks about. It was his testimony in one song. As I started singing a little of it, he joined in. It was a hoot! Let's just say his singing skills weren't quite as developed as his basketball skills. (I'm just glad he didn't ask me to dribble!) After the sound check we had some time before the athletes arrived and he gave me a personal tour of the athletic dorm he lived in as a student years before. He shared how this trip was his first one back to campus since leaving (something the local papers had written extensively about). He went on to say that some had speculated he had not returned because LSU fired his father as basketball coach the year after he left. He told me that wasn't it at all. "I was ashamed of the person I had been and the way I treated people while I was here," he explained.

Later that night in the program, I decided on the spur of the moment to sing "Oh Buddah" for the crowd and called Pete up to sing it with me. "Pistol" stepped right up and joined me. The place went wild! Then he humbly gave his testimony about the difference Christ had made in his life. Many young men gave their heart to the Lord that night.

Just a few weeks later Pete collapsed while playing basketball with James Dobson of Focus on the Family. When the story of his death hit the news, I wept, thinking about what he said that night just a few weeks before. He told all of us that he had tried to fill his life with basketball and fame and it didn't work. Then he tried drugs and euphoric experiences and it didn't work. He turned to every religion under the sun and none of them filled the emptiness of his life. Only when he came to Christ and opened his heart up to the Savior did he learn that his heart had been made to be the dwelling place of God. Only Jesus could fill the place built just for Him. He asked Jesus into his heart and the Lord came in and filled his life with meaning and purpose. Pete learned an important truth about worship: the heart was built to be the dwelling place of the Lord.

The mystery of the ages has been revealed: God is in us and among us. And His presence is available every time we worship Him—wherever we may be.

In the Gospel of John, Jesus made it clear that He was the One who came to establish relationship with God's people in order for true worship to occur. He spoke these words:

> "But an hour is coming, and is now here, when the true worshipers will worship the Father in spirit and truth. Yes, the Father wants such people to worship Him. God is spirit, and those who worship Him must worship in spirit and truth." (John 4:23–24)

Jesus knew that the Father had sent Him to redeem mankind—and to precede the coming of the Holy Spirit, who would reside in the hearts of all believers. God was about to "build" a new temple in the hearts of His people, and that would become a new place of worship. The time had come for true worshippers to be empowered to worship in spirit and truth!

You see, God created us for worship. Just as surely as He delivered the Hebrew nation from bondage in Egypt and provided a pathway to the Promised Land, God sent Jesus to redeem us and make a way for us to enter God's presence. That Way is Jesus Himself—the Way, the Truth, and the Life.

> Jesus told him, "I am the way, the truth, and the life. No one comes to the Father except through Me." (John 14:6)

Jesus declared a new covenant that could never be broken. His blood was shed in order that we might be redeemed and receive the indwelling Spirit of God. We are the temple, the holy place of God's Spirit. When we gather, we know that He is present, just as He was present whenever His people worshipped in the Old Testament:

> "Our forefathers had the tabernacle of the testimony in the desert, just as He who spoke to Moses commanded him to make it according to the pattern he had seen. Our forefathers in turn received it and with Joshua brought it in when they dispossessed the nations that God drove out before our fathers, until the days of David. He found favor in God's sight and asked that he might provide a dwelling place for the God of Jacob. But it was Solomon who built Him a house. However, the Most High does not dwell in sanctuaries made with hands, as the prophet says:

"Heaven is My throne, and earth My footstool.
What sort of house will you build for Me?" says the Lord,
"or what is My resting place?
Did not My hand make all these things?" (Acts 7:44–50)

Call to Worship

When we are alone, we can still worship because He has chosen to dwell with us and in us. This is the divine mystery that was hidden from the ages—Christ in us, the hope of glory.

We were indeed created for worship. A lifetime of mistakes and failures can't change that. Circumstances—good or bad—can't change that. There is a deep need within each of us to know our Creator, recognize His goodness to us, and come into His holy presence to receive from His gracious hand of mercy. He alone is worthy!

Reflections

- In the Old Testament, God chose to meet with His people in the tabernacle and later in the temple.
- Today we have access to God through Jesus—and Him alone.
- Jesus' blood was shed in order that we might be redeemed and receive the indwelling Spirit of God. We are the temple, the holy place, of God's Spirit.
- Because of Christ Jesus and His sacrifice for our sins, we can come freely into God's presence. Our past failures and sins do not limit our freedom to worship God.

Prayer

Jesus, thank You for Your willingness to die on a cross
in my place. Help me understand how to respond to
such love and sacrifice for me. Amen.

GRACE

Song of Worship

"Shadow of Your Cross"

Lamb of God, Son of Man
How You suffered, how You bled
With a crown of thorns pressed upon Your head
You chose the road of pain
You walked the hill of all my shame
All my shame

Man of sorrows, crucified
Pure and holy sacrifice
As the hammer hit the nail, You offered up Your life
You gave up heaven for Your own
You took our punishment alone
You were so alone

(Chorus)
In the shadow of Your cross I will live for all my days
How could I forget the price You paid
In the shelter of Your love I will give You all my praise
In the shadow of Your cross I will stay

—WORDS AND MUSIC BY JOEL ENGLE
COPYRIGHT 2005 SPIN THREE-SIXTY MUSIC/BMI
(ADMIN. BY MUSIC SERVICES, NASHVILLE)

Amazing Grace

Each of us was **created** by God for relationship with Him, but we can only enjoy that relationship by God's **grace**.

Entering God's presence requires grace that only He can provide.

God is serious about having a relationship with us and being our first priority in life. As we have seen, He continually told the Israelites, "I am the LORD your God." He brought them out of bondage in Egypt; kept them fed and clothed for forty years; and led them into a land that He had set aside for them. And they responded to God's grace with great love, appreciation, obedience, and worship—well, not exactly!

In fact, they didn't respond well at all. They grumbled and complained and worshipped other gods. Even while Moses was on Mount Sinai interceding with God on their behalf, they were creating a golden calf to

Read More about It

- "I am the LORD your God": Exodus 6:7; 16:12; 20:2; Deuteronomy 5:6
- Deliverance from Egypt: Acts 7:35–36
- 40 years in the desert: Deuteronomy 2:7; 8:2–4; 29:5
- Clothed and fed in the wilderness: Exodus 15:22–27; 16–17:7
- Claiming the promised land: Numbers 33:50–53; Joshua 1:1–5

worship. Yet God would not forsake His people—then or now. God was determined to show His grace and the holiness of His great name through His people, and He intends to do the same in our generation.

Becoming Aware of God's Grace

The Israelites weren't all that different from us today. Many times God is demonstrating His great grace in our lives, and, frankly, we just don't get it! I vividly remember when Teresa and I encountered God's grace in that way. God's grace was flowing with great power toward us, but we just couldn't see it at first.

The doctors later called it a medical fluke, but we knew better. Teresa had noticed something that later would be diagnosed as breast cancer. As you can imagine, it really was a shock and very frightening to both of us, but our doctor wasn't concerned in the least. He didn't even think a biopsy was needed.

Initially, I agreed with the doctor and tried to calm Teresa's concerns. I just didn't want to put my wife—the treasure of my life—and cancer in the same sentence, much less the same physical body.

It wasn't an easy time, and to make matters worse, once Teresa began to agree with the doctor and me that there really was no need for a biopsy, I began to argue that she *really did need one!* We went back and forth, back and forth, and finally the doctor agreed to perform the procedure as one of those necessary precautions to give us peace of mind.

As it turned out, the biopsy *was* necessary! And the decision we made to have the biopsy most likely saved her life. It was a life-and-death decision, and the intervention of the Holy Spirit led us to make the right choice.

Teresa is living proof that God's grace is sufficient, and that He actively pursues His people. God knows exactly what we need for every situation we encounter, and He wants to direct our steps, showering us with His grace all along the way. But first we must become aware of God's grace and then choose to respond.

> A man's heart plans his way, but the LORD determines his steps. (Prov. 16:9)

Grace: The Unmerited Favor of God.

As noted in the *Holman Illustrated Bible Dictionary*, the Hebrew words used for *grace* are *chen* (n.) and *chanan* (v.), and they mean "grace" or "favor" and "to be gracious, to show favor," respectively.[1] These words express a divine-human relationship whereby the lesser human receives undeserved or unmerited favor at the hands of the superior God.

Grace forms the basis for all of God's relationship with man and His activity on behalf of man. The Bible is filled with example after example. Just consider this short list from the Old Testament alone:

Grace delivered Noah and his family from the flood (see Gen. 6:5–8).

Grace delivered Lot from destruction at Sodom and Gomorrah (see Gen. 19:15–19).

Grace gave Moses a personal knowledge of God and His ways (see Exod. 33:12–13).

Grace assured Moses of God's presence with Israel and His forgiveness of their sin (see Exod. 33:17; 34:9).

Grace caused Moses to see the glory of God (see Exod. 33:18–23).

Grace chose Israel for God's inheritance (see Exod. 33:16).

Grace preserved the remnant from captivity (see Ezra 9:8).[2]

God did all this and so much more for the Israelites, but often they just didn't get it. We in the church today are often in danger of missing it as well. Though we know of Christ's life, death, and resurrection, we often fail to grasp or truly appreciate the depth of God's amazing grace. Pause just a moment and think about this statement:

The sovereign God of the universe reached down from His holy throne and took on real flesh and blood in order to redeem sinners like you and me.

That is unmerited favor and an act of overwhelming kindness on His part. God really has made you and me alive—alive forever!

And you were dead in your trespasses and sins . . . so that in the coming ages He might display the immeasurable riches of His grace in His kindness to us in Christ Jesus. For by grace you are saved through faith, and this is not from yourselves; it is God's gift—not from works, so that no one can boast. (Eph. 2:1, 7–9)

Grace: The Transforming Power of God

But God doesn't leave us there at the moment of salvation to work out the rest of life on our own. Instead, He provides grace, which is His transforming power to grow us into His likeness, to bring us to the fullness of His glory, day by day, as we submit our lives to Him.

We all, with unveiled faces, are reflecting the glory of the Lord and are being transformed into the same image from glory to glory; this is from the Lord who is the Spirit. (2 Cor. 3:18)

Therefore since we have a great high priest who has passed through the heavens—Jesus the Son of God—let us hold fast to the confession. For we do not have a high priest who is unable to sympathize with our weaknesses, but One who has been tested in every way as we are, yet without sin. Therefore let us approach the throne of grace with boldness, so that we may receive mercy and find grace to help us at the proper time. (Heb. 4:14–16)

When I was a sophomore in high school God's grace was at work in my life in an unusual way, though at the time I thought the worst possible thing had happened to me. My parents moved our family into a new house. No big deal, right? Wrong!

You see, our new house was in a different school district. I was playing football and baseball for Corinth High School and was all set for a great junior year starting in both sports. But then we learned that since I was living outside the district, I would not be eligible to play for my school. I could transfer to the school in the district I was living in and play right away; but if I remained a student at Corinth High School, I would have to sit out a year. I just couldn't leave all my team-mates and friends so I was sunk—and mad! Our coaches went crazy! I was a starting pitcher and was supposed to be the starting quarter-back. One coach even offered to let me live with him for the year just so I could remain eligible. (My mom loved that one.) The coaches appealed to the state office but the appeal was denied. I was ineligible to play for one year. I fumed and fussed and wallowed in my anger at God. After all, I was going to be a professional athlete who made a difference for Him. How could He let this happen? My life felt like it was ruined.

During my junior year I had plenty of time on my hands since there were no football practices after school and I absolutely hated going and sitting on the sidelines. At my parent's insistence, I started taking piano lessons. My other option was working more at my dad's store, so I chose piano! I also started playing guitar more and more. Then I started writing songs and singing more. My life began to have a different focus. I didn't know it, but my future life was under development during this year I thought was going to be a waste of time. When my senior year finally came, I was right back on the football team and baseball team and eventually played baseball in college. But something strange happened during my junior year without sports. I began to look at life a little differently. When the time came later to walk away from baseball and focus on ministry, it was somehow easy to do. I had learned that my life was about much more than sports. And, I had learned to love singing and writing songs about my faith. That summer after my junior year was when I sang my first original song at Ridgecrest. It was a life-changing year to say the least.

God had used a hard circumstance to work in my life and prepare me for a future ministry focus. His transforming grace was doing His work, even while I was kicking and screaming.

In the New Testament, particularly in the apostle Paul's letters to the churches, grace is defined by the Greek word *charis*. In the book of Acts, *charis* is used to refer to the grace-filled power that flowed from God or the exalted Christ to both unbelievers and believers. It is God's *charis*, God's grace, that gave unbelievers the power to believe, believers the ability to be built up or transformed, and the apostles the capability to be successful in their mission.

Read More about It

- Grace reveals Christ and gives faith (condition of salvation): Acts 18:27; Galatians 1:6; Ephesians 2:8–9; Philippians 1:29
- Grace calls and equips believers for Christian service: Acts 4:33; 11:23; 13:43; 14:26; 20:32; Romans 15:15–16; 1 Corinthians 3:10

Paul was so aware of the grace of God in his own life that he refers to it at the beginning and end of every one of his letters. The grace of God in Paul's life was something that was always with him, producing labor, humility, and goodness and sustaining him in times of difficulty. For him, the Christian life was summed up in the grace of God—unmerited favor and transforming power for every believer.

Read More about It

- God's grace in Paul's life: 1 Corinthians 15:10; 2 Corinthians 1:12; 12:7–10

God's grace always has been sufficient, always is sufficient, and always will be sufficient for everything we face in this life. And He is worthy of our worship—always! Grace is indeed the unmerited favor that only God can provide—and the transforming power of God for every person and every issue of life. But, just like the Israelites, it is always our decision to respond.

Preparing to Worship

As we have seen, God was present throughout the Israelites' journey. He made it clear: "I will dwell among the Israelites and be their God" (Exod. 29:45). God even commanded Moses to build a place where He could dwell among them:

> "They are to make a sanctuary for Me so that I may dwell among them." (Exod. 25:8 NKJV)

Still, the people could not enter God's presence. Although they were created to enjoy intimate relationship with God, their rebellion made it impossible for them to have direct contact with Him.

Scripture indicates that only well-prepared priests could approach God and come into His presence, and they could do so only once a year. These priests prepared extensively for their encounter with the Holy One of Israel. They knew that they were not worthy of God's presence, and that every detail of cleansing and sacrifice was crucial if they were to survive their trip inside the holy of holies. Do you recall some of the rituals the priests had to carry out? Try to imagine yourself fulfilling even this brief list of practices they had to endure:

- They had to wear the sacred garments whenever they entered the tent of meeting so they wouldn't incur guilt and die (see Exod. 28:2–43).
- They had to be consecrated in a very specific manner to serve as priests (see Exod. 29:1–46; Lev. 8:1–36).
- They had to burn fragrant incense on the altar every morning and evening (see Exod. 30:7–8).
- They had to wash their hands and feet with water from the sacred basin (see Exod. 30:19–21).
- They had to make atonement annually with the blood of the "atoning sin offering" (see Exod. 30:10).

All this and much more was required for them to enter the presence of the same God who makes Himself readily available to every believer today. *Entering the presence of God is still a very serious matter—and grace makes it all possible!*

Call to Worship

Do you do anything special to prepare for worship—a private time, maybe at home, or a prayer time at your church? If you answered no to this question, you are not alone. Many times overcoming the distractions and difficulties of actually having a private time of worship or simply getting to church crowds out our focus on the actual worship opportunity we are about to encounter.

Here is a list of ways that could potentially help you prepare for worship:

- Pray before every worship experience. When worshipping privately, make prayer the first thing you do. When preparing for a corporate worship service, pray as you're getting ready for the service, traveling to the service, and/or waiting for the service to begin.
- Play worship music throughout your home while getting ready for church and in the car on the way. Make music part of your private worship times as well.
- Keep a journal of what God has done in your life and refer to it often. Remember, worship is our response to who God is and what He has done! So write down the ways that God reveals Himself and His activity in your life, and review the impact of God's grace in your life often.
- As you prepare for private worship or a church service, begin to expect that you will encounter God in a personal way. Allow expectation to grow in your heart!

Reflections

- God was present with the Israelites throughout their forty years in the desert.
- God provided the people a way to encounter His presence through priests who endured extensive ritualistic preparations in order to enter the holy of holies.
- Today God's grace alone makes it possible for us to enter His presence!
- Many times we don't immediately recognize God's grace working in our lives, but God's grace is always there.

Prayer

*Lord, thank You for the hard lessons that help me
know You more. Give me the grace to understand that
You are always near and always working in my life,
no matter the circumstance. Amen.*

Notes

1. *Holman Illustrated Bible Dictionary* (Nashville: B&H Publishing Group, 2003).

2. Ibid.

3. Ibid.

12

God's Ultimate Expression of Grace

*God's grace comes to us through
the shed blood of Jesus Christ.*

God's amazing grace comes through the shed blood of Jesus Christ and is available to all who receive Him as Lord and Savior. Our personal relationship with Jesus allows us to encounter His presence with faith and confidence and, as a result, to experience God in worship. The writer of the book of Hebrews expresses it this way:

> Therefore, brothers, since we have boldness to enter the sanctuary through the blood of Jesus, by the new and living way that He has inaugurated for us, through the curtain (that is, His flesh); and since we have a great high priest over the house of God, let us draw near with a true heart in full assurance of faith, our hearts sprinkled clean from an evil conscience and our bodies washed in pure water. (Heb. 10:19–22)

We have seen that the only access God's people had to the holy of holies, where God's presence dwelt and where the highest form of worship took place, was through the high priest. But when Jesus, our High Priest, came, He entered the most holy place once and for all by His own blood, obtaining our eternal redemption:

> How much more will the blood of the Messiah, who through the eternal Spirit offered Himself without blemish to God, cleanse our consciences from dead works to serve the living God? (Heb. 9:14)

We just can't miss this truth: All of us who have accepted Jesus as Lord and Savior are received into God's presence through the One who purchased us with His blood. No amount of ritualistic cleansing or devoted actions could prepare us for God's presence—and none is needed!

God came down to us in Christ Jesus. He is the spotless Lamb of God who was slain for our sins and our inequities. There is no further need for sacrifice; the price of sin has been paid in full. We are no longer separated from the presence of God.

> Suddenly, the curtain of the sanctuary was split in two from top to bottom; the earth quaked and the rocks were split. (Matt. 27:51)

The commentary on this verse in the *MacArthur Study Bible* offers this explanation: "The tearing of the veil signified that the way into God's presence was now open to all through a new and living way. . . . The fact that it tore from top to bottom showed that no man had split the veil. God did it."[1]

Here's a statement that will help you grasp this truth once and forever:

> Jesus *broke down* the barrier so you could *break through* whatever holds you back and allow Him to *break in* to the *broken places* in your life.

This is pure grace! We deserved to die in our sins, but God made a way—a way for us to experience His very presence in our lives—a way to join Him in the most holy place. Our only reasonable response is worship. And as we worship—as we break through traditions, doubts, and fears that have restricted our worship expression—God Himself has promised to be present. And when the King is present, all things are possible.

We Are Worthy of His Presence

Most of us have read what the Bible clearly says about who we are in Christ, yet many of us have missed the reality of what is being said. Throughout my lifetime, I've heard "good Christian folks" refer to themselves (with good intentions) as "just an old sinner, saved by grace." The Bible makes it clear: if you have accepted Jesus Christ as Lord and Savior, you *are* saved by grace!

You might have *been* an "old sinner," but you aren't any longer. By grace and grace alone, you are a new creation, fully righteous in God's eyes. To believe and say anything else simply contradicts what God has proclaimed in His Word about you. Jesus' sacrifice at Calvary really did tear apart any barrier between you and God. You are free to enter God's presence and worship Him freely!

> *Therefore, if anyone is in Christ, he is a new creation; old things have passed away; behold, all things have become new. (2 Cor. 5:17 NKJV)*

There are undoubtedly many good things one could say about you. Look at the attributes in the following list and see if they might apply to your life. Would any one of these grant you entrance into the presence of Holy God?

- Friendly (and a faithful friend to others)
- Kind
- Generous (freely give your time and resources to others)
- Temperate (not given to anger)
- Forgiving
- Devoted (to friends and family)
- Successful (at work, at home, etc.)
- Well-to-do (plentiful financial resources)
- Honest
- Humble
- Good character
- Servant (in church, community, elsewhere)
- Other

Let's take a look at the following verses in light of the attributes above:

> *But God, who is abundant in mercy, because of His great love that He had for us, made us alive with the Messiah even*

*though we were dead in trespasses. By grace you are saved!
He also raised us up with Him and seated us with Him in the
heavens, in Christ Jesus, so that in the coming ages He might
display the immeasurable riches of His grace in His kindness
to us in Christ Jesus. For by grace you are saved through
faith, and this is not from yourselves; it is God's gift—not from
works, so that no one can boast. For we are His creation—
created in Christ Jesus for good works, which God prepared
ahead of time so that we should walk in them. (Eph. 2:4–10)*

All these attributes are simply "good works, which God prepared
ahead of time so that [you] should walk in them" (Eph. 2:10), but they
are completely insufficient to grant you access to God! Of course, God
is serious about good works. In fact, the entire Bible is designed to
"thoroughly equip" us for every good work:

*All Scripture is given by inspiration of God, and is profitable
for doctrine, for reproof, for correction, for instruction in righteousness, that the man of God may be complete, thoroughly
equipped for every good work. (2 Tim. 3:16–17 NKJV)*

But works are never enough. We are qualified for His glorious
presence by grace and grace alone.

Call to Worship

It is absolutely crucial that you settle the issue of worth once and
for all: If you have accepted Jesus as Lord and Savior, no further qualification is necessary for you to enter the presence of Holy God. There
is no amount of work you can do to improve on this absolute truth—
salvation comes by grace and grace alone.

To further settle this truth in your mind, take a moment to remember any major failures in your life—but don't dwell on them. Now,
compare the list of "good" and "bad" for a brief moment. Can your
good works every really overcome the weight of your sin? Of course
not! Grace is our only means to worship our holy God, and aren't
we glad!

Reflections

- Grace came down to us in Christ Jesus—the spotless Lamb of God—who was sacrificed as full payment for the penalty of our sins and sinful nature.
- No other sacrifice is necessary for us to be worthy of God's presence.
- No amount of works or proper behavior on our part will ever qualify us for God's presence—only the shed blood of Jesus Christ.

Prayer

Jesus, thank You for the cross and for the death You died so that I could know life in You. Amen.

Notes

1. *The MacArthur Study Bible* (Nashville: Word Publishing, 1997).

13

Accepting God's Gift of Grace

Salvation is a matter of accepting God's gift of grace by faith.

Amazing grace! How sweet the sound that saved a wretch like me.
I once was lost, but now am found; was blind, but now I see.[1]

After spending my whole adult life in church leadership, I know firsthand just how easy it is to sing this hymn yet not be convinced that the message is completely true on a personal level. The Bible is filled with standards, principles, and challenges that call believers like you and me to live a godly life—and we often fall short of perfection. As a result, there are many in the church today who carry an unspoken concern that maybe, just maybe, there is something else they must do to be fully His.

Believe—Belong—Become

Often the unstated message of the church today goes like this:

If you *believe*, and if you *behave*, then you can *belong*.

The Bible, however, presents a different message:

If you *believe*, then you *belong* to Christ; and you can *become* the person God created you to be.

As we make a conscious decision to embrace God's Word by faith—to *believe* what it says about Jesus and receive Him as our Lord and Savior—we truly *belong* to Him! Then as we put our faith into action and begin to follow the instructions God provides in His written Word, we really can *become* the persons we were designed to be, as the following verses affirm:

> *All Scripture is inspired by God and is profitable for teaching, for rebuking, for correcting, for training in righteousness, so that the man of God may be complete, equipped for every good work. (2 Tim. 3:16–17)*
>
> *Therefore, ridding yourselves of all moral filth and evil excess, humbly receive the **implanted** word, which is able to save you. (James 1:21, emphasis added)*

Implant[ed]—fix[ed] or set securely or deeply; set permanently in the consciousness or habit patterns.[2]

Once we *believe*, we really do *belong*. And in order to *become*, we simply must walk in the light we have been given through God's Word, fellowshipping with one another, confessing our sins, and setting our minds on things of the Spirit rather than on things of the flesh. As we read in the book of Hebrews:

> *Let us hold on to the confession of our hope without wavering, for He who promised is faithful. And let us be concerned about one another in order to promote love and good works, not staying away from our meetings, as some habitually do, but encouraging each other, and all the more as you see the day drawing near. (Heb. 10:23–25)*

Today Is the Day

If there is any doubt in your mind that you have received God's ultimate gift of grace by accepting Jesus as Lord and Savior of your own life, today is the day to settle the matter once and for all. Jesus Christ, the Son of God, came to Earth in order to make a way for you to be reconciled to God. It doesn't matter what you have done or where you have been. Jesus is waiting to receive you right now.

The first question you must answer is this: Do I need a Savior, or is my life sufficient to obtain eternal life with God by its own merit? In other words, is there any other way to get to God?

Jesus made clear that He is the only way to the Father—the only way to living an abundant life now and spending eternity in the presence of Almighty God:

> Jesus told him, "I am the way, the truth, and the life. No one comes to the Father except through Me." (John 14:6)

Your salvation truly is a matter of life and death.

If you agree that you need a Savior today, He is available. Jesus is ready right now to welcome you into His glorious kingdom. And the Bible is clear about how this happens: if you believe in your heart that Jesus is the Son of God who was raised from the dead and if you confess with your mouth that Jesus is Lord, you *will* be saved.

> The message is near you, in your mouth and in your heart. This is the message of faith that we proclaim: if you confess with your mouth, "Jesus is Lord," and believe in your heart that God raised Him from the dead, you will be saved. (Rom. 10:8–9)

> For by grace you are saved through faith, and this is not from yourselves; it is God's gift—not from works, so that no one can boast. (Eph. 2:8–9)

If you have any doubt about your salvation, you can be born of the Spirit right now, and you will never have to wonder again. You will be a new creation.

> Therefore if anyone is in Christ, there is a new creation; old things have passed away, and look, new things have come. Now everything is from God, who has reconciled us to Himself through Christ. (2 Cor. 5:17–18)

Jesus not only made it clear that no one comes to the Father except through Him; He also told us that no one comes to Him unless the Father draws that person to Him.

Jesus answered them, "Stop complaining among yourselves. No one can come to Me unless the Father who sent Me draws him, and I will raise him up on the last day." (John 6:43–44)

And the fact that you are drawn to Jesus is a clear indication that the Father has determined this is the day you are to repent of your sins—turn from them—and receive Jesus as Lord. You can give Jesus the controls of your life.

Years ago I was blessed to have a friend named Ray who was the pilot of the company plane for a large corporation. He had offered on several occasions to fly me anywhere in the country if I ever had a problem getting somewhere. One day I took him up on the offer. He picked me up at the small airfield in Dayton, Tennessee, to fly me home from a youth conference I had led the week before at Bryan College. I was enjoying the flight and fellowship in the copilot's seat on the plush King Air plane. Then Ray asked me an interesting question. "You want to fly the plane?" I gave an interesting answer; "Sure." And Ray began to coach me on how to fly while we were at 20,000 feet. It was a blast! Before long, I started getting the hang of it. As we were getting closer and closer to the airport, I began to wonder just when he wanted the controls back. He kept telling me what to do and I kept doing it.

Before long he said, "You want to land it?" I said, "You're kidding! There's no way I can land this plane!" "Sure you can," Ray said. "You've been doing great. You're following directions well and you've got a good feel of the plane. I believe you can do it. Come on. Give it a try." As he kept talking to the control tower, I followed every direction and finally lined us up on final approach—2,000 feet, 1,500 feet, 1,000 feet—the ground was getting closer and closer and my heart was pounding more and more! Ray said "If you get uncomfortable, just take your hands off the wheel and I'll take it from there." My hands were sweating and my heart was racing—500 feet . . . Finally, just a couple of hundred feet off the ground, I took my hands off the wheel and shouted "I can't do it!" Ray took the controls and calmly landed the plane and I could breathe again.

Living life without Christ is like trying to fly your own plane without a license. While you're in the air, it may feel like you are in control; but because of sin, you can't land this plane. One of these days at the end of life, your plane will lose altitude and start going down. What will you do then? You can't land your plane, and deep in your heart you know that. You've somehow thought that you could fly so well in the air that the landing will just work out at the end. Wrong. It doesn't work that way. Jesus is the only one who can land the plane. The old bumper sticker says, "God is my copilot." I beg to differ. God is the pilot! Crying out to Him for His salvation is like taking your hands off the controls and trusting Him to land your plane. He's ready when you are. Take your hands off the controls right now and place your trust in Him.

You *can* exchange your life of sin and failure for His life of righteousness and favor with God and man right now! Please read and repeat aloud the prayer of salvation at the end of today's reading. Be sure to tell someone you know who is a Christian about your decision so that he or she may help you walk out the next steps of your life in Christ.

Your Salvation Is Secure

If you have already accepted Jesus Christ yet continue to have nagging doubts about your salvation, He wants to give you unshakable confidence and peace in knowing that your salvation is secure. You don't have to be a habitual criminal or trapped in some diabolical sin pattern to doubt your salvation and position in Christ. In fact, many Christians carry around a nagging concern about their salvation, wondering if they "measure up." But as we have seen, there is no way to work your way to salvation. Salvation is a matter of grace and faith alone. It is available by the grace of God and is received by your faith in Jesus Christ as Lord of your life.

If you are one who continues to struggle with doubts about your salvation, it is imperative that you read and believe this passage from the book of Romans:

> What then are we to say about these things? If God is for us, who is against us? He did not even spare His own Son, but offered Him up for us all; how will He not also with Him grant us everything? Who can bring an accusation against God's elect? God is the One who justifies. Who is the one who condemns? Christ Jesus is the One who died, but even more, has been raised; He also is at the right hand of God and intercedes for us. Who can separate us from the love of Christ? Can affliction or anguish or persecution or famine or nakedness or danger or sword? As it is written:

"Because of You we are being put to death all day long;
we are counted as sheep to be slaughtered."
No, in all these things we are more than victorious
through Him who loved us. For I am persuaded that neither
death nor life, nor angels nor rulers, nor things present, nor
things to come, nor powers, nor height, nor depth, nor any
other created thing will have the power to separate us from
the love of God that is in Christ Jesus our Lord!
(Rom. 8:31–39)

Call to Worship

Romans 10:17 tells us that "faith comes by hearing and hearing by the word of God" (NKJV). As you declare the Word of God aloud, it will enter your heart and your faith will be strengthened. Once Jesus is Lord of your life, you can have confidence that you are always saved. And as Romans 8:38–39 assures us, *nothing* can ever separate us from the love of God. Now that is revelation!

Jesus is indeed Lord of your life, and He will never, ever leave you or forsake you. As you meditate for a few minutes on who He is and what He has already done, worship will be your only reasonable and adequate response!

Reflections

- Jesus is the only way to the Father—both now and throughout eternity.
- Personal salvation and a relationship with God through Jesus Christ are available to all who believe.
- Salvation is a matter of grace and faith—we believe Jesus is the Son of God and confess Him as Lord of our lives, and by God's grace we are granted entrance into the kingdom of God now and forever.
- Once Jesus is Lord of your life, you can have confidence that you are always saved.
- Nothing can ever separate us from the love of God!

Prayer

*Heavenly Father, I come to You in the name of Jesus.
Your Word says that if I confess with my mouth the
Lord Jesus and believe in my heart that God has raised
Him from the dead, I will be saved. I take You at Your word,
Lord God. I confess that Jesus is Lord, and I believe
in my heart that You raised Him from the dead.
I invite You to be Lord of my life, and I thank You for
coming into my heart and giving me Your Holy Spirit as
You promised. I believe in You and Your Son, Jesus Christ,
and I commit the rest of my life to You this very day.
God, I praise You for Your awesome love! Thank You for
reaching all the way to me and for promising You will never
leave. I rest today in Your promise! Amen.*

Notes

1. John Newton, 1779.

2. *Merriam-Webster* online dictionary (www.m-w.com/dictionary/implanted).

14

Worship in Spirit and Truth

True worship is expressed through spirit and truth—
our spirit surrendered to God's Truth.

In the Gospel of John, we read the story of a Samaritan woman who encountered Jesus, the Lamb of God. We know her as the woman at the well. Isn't it interesting that when this woman realized she was in the presence of someone very special, she immediately turned the conversation to worship!

> "Sir," the woman replied, "I see that You are a prophet. Our fathers worshiped on this mountain, yet you Jews say that the place to worship is in Jerusalem." (John 4:19–20)

Jesus used this encounter to explain what God requires of us as we worship—even today. The woman knew enough about worship to ask Jesus about the right *location*, but He responded with a message about the right *relationship*—the relationship between God and the worshipper. Jesus clearly taught that the condition of the worshipper's heart is always God's primary interest and the only requirement for true worship.

Jesus told her, "Believe Me, woman, an hour is coming when
you will worship the Father neither on this mountain nor in
Jerusalem. . . . But an hour is coming, and is now here, when
the true worshipers will worship the Father in spirit and truth.
Yes, the Father wants such people to worship Him. God is
spirit, and those who worship Him must worship in spirit and
truth." (John 4:21, 23–24)

Jesus' words to the Samaritan woman at the well ring loudly to all believers—that the place of worship no longer had to be the temple in Jerusalem—or the cathedral or the sanctuary of First Church. No matter where our place of worship may be, we can offer the Father the worship He desires as long as it flows from deep within our surrendered hearts.

Worshipping in Spirit

God is not impressed with outward expressions of worship that do not come from our surrendered and grateful hearts, no matter how excellent we may think our expressions of worship are. True worship comes from within, as this verse implies:

"These people honor Me with their lips, but their heart is far
from Me. They worship Me in vain." (Matt. 15:8–9)

Worship that meets man's "performance standard" is not the issue. God hears and receives only what is offered to Him in spirit. He is the One who sets the standard of performance that matters. True worship is expressed through spirit and truth: our spirit surrendered to His Truth. Jesus established that anything less is unacceptable.

I'm ashamed of the fact that in my earlier years in music ministry, there would not have been room for Seth in my choir. You see, Seth was a wonderful man—probably in his late thirties at the time—who loved God and loved to sing. But Seth lived with Down's syndrome. Seth could sing on pitch, but he couldn't harmonize with the other tenors.

He simply would not have passed my "performance standard" as a young music minister. But Seth passed the only standard that mattered: he was a worshipper of the Living God, who worshipped with all his heart—and God knew it!

Seth fit right in with our music team from the beginning. When he sang, he sang with joy on his face like no one else in the choir. Down's syndrome could not steal Seth's revelation of who God is and what He had done in Seth's life! Seth sang with joy on his face and tears streaming down his cheeks. His unashamed worship of His Savior challenged all of us to the core.

God used Seth in my life to secure this truth forever: people look at the outward expression of worship—what we see and hear—but God always looks at the inner heart of the worshipper.

> *"Man does not see what the LORD sees, for man sees what is visible, but the LORD sees the heart." (1 Sam. 16:7)*

Seth worshipped in spirit—and in truth—and God chose to dwell there with him.

The indwelling of the Holy Spirit is what makes it possible for us to worship the Father in spirit. Although human beings can reproduce human life, it takes the Spirit of God to breathe divine life into the spirit of a man or a woman:

> *"Whatever is born of the flesh is flesh, and whatever is born of the Spirit is spirit." (John 3:6)*

Worshipping the Father in spirit, then, begins with being born again. Salvation, a divine gift of grace, opens the doorway to the relationship that God deeply desires. The power and presence of the Spirit resides in every heart surrendered to the lordship of Jesus. And that Spirit of the Living God invites the spirit within each of us to worship from a pure heart.

Read More about It

- The New Covenant: Hebrews 8:6; 10:16; 13:20–21

Worshipping in Truth

True worshippers worship the Father not only in spirit, but also in truth. Jesus is the Truth. He said, "I am the way, the truth, and the life. No one comes to the Father except through Me" (John 14:6). All who worship the Father must do so through Jesus. Worship under the New Covenant is through Christ, in Christ, and for Christ. Therefore, as the writer of the book of Hebrews encourages us,

Therefore, through Him let us continually offer up to God a
sacrifice of praise, that is, the fruit of our lips that confess His
name. (Heb. 13:15)

The Truth is a person, and His name is Jesus. True worship is always our response to His revelation.

God provided Jesus, the Living Word, to establish once and forever a secure foundation of true worship for us. You see, we must have a revelation of God—a correct view of God *in relationship to who we are*—if we are to worship the Father in truth, and His Word always provides such a view. God has never changed, and He never will.

Jesus is the perfect expression of the nature and character of God. God is fully revealed in Jesus, and Jesus is the one and only Truth:

In these last days, [God] has spoken to us by His Son . . . [who]
is the radiance of His glory, the exact expression of His nature,
and He sustains all things by His powerful word . . . He sat
down at the right hand of the Majesty on high. (Heb. 1:2–3)

Worship that is Christ-centered and Christ-focused is true worship, and worship that comes from a heart filled with Jesus, the Living Word, will never be in vain. Location is not what matters most to God. What matters to God is that we worship in spirit and truth.

Call to Worship

Jesus said it is now time to worship the Father in *spirit* and *truth*. And the grace of God expressed in Christ Jesus is the only thing that allows you and me access to the Father.

Worshipping in spirit is characterized by worship that comes from the innermost part of our hearts—hearts that are filled with awe and appreciation that can only come from our personal and intimate encounter with the Lord.

Worshipping in truth occurs as we worship with an understanding of who God truly is and who we are by comparison. (We will explore our position relative to God in detail in the next chapter.) God and all His attributes are fully revealed in Jesus Christ, who is the Truth. As Jesus proclaimed: it is time to worship Him in spirit and in truth! And grace makes it all possible.

Reflections

- Jesus used the Samaritan woman to draw an *entire village* to Himself! Many believed and were saved.
- True worship is expressed through spirit and truth: our spirit surrendered to God's truth. Anything less is unacceptable.
- God is more interested in the condition of the worshipper's heart than in any outward expression of worship or place of worship. God's only requirement for true worship is a surrendered heart.
- We must be born again in order to worship God in spirit.
- God is fully revealed in Jesus; Jesus is the Truth, the true Living Word. Worship is our response to His revelation!

Prayer

Lord Jesus, forgive me for those times I have focused on the external aspects of worship. I know You see into my heart. Help me bring a heart of worship before You. Amen.

15

A Correct View of God

*True worship requires that we understand who God is
and who we are in comparison.*

Throughout the first part of this book, we developed two basic points:

1. Worship is our response to God's revelation of who He is and what He has done.
2. Our worship provides a place of meeting, a habitation for God's presence.

Worship is fairly simple: God initiates and we respond. Yet as we respond, it is crucial that we understand who God is, who we are in relation to Him, how we should respond, and what we can expect. The prophet Isaiah provides us with a clear understanding of each of these points.

Isaiah's Revelation

Isaiah was called by God to prophesy to the nation of Israel from 739 to 686 BC. It was a very dark period for Israel. Although Isaiah knew from the beginning that his ministry would be one of fruitless warning and exhortation, he responded (see Isa. 6:9–13). However, Isaiah's words burned brightly for the early church, which is evidenced by the fact that Isaiah is quoted more than sixty-five different times in the New Testament.

Isaiah's words provide clear understanding for believers today as well. His vision of the throne of God, in particular, clarifies who God is, who we are, how we should respond, and what we can expect. In the sixth chapter, he wrote:

> In the year that King Uzziah died, I saw the Lord seated
> on a high and lofty throne, and His robe filled the temple.
> Seraphim were standing above Him; each one had six wings:
> with two he covered his face, with two he covered his feet,
> and with two he flew. And one called to another:
> Holy, holy, holy is the LORD of Hosts;
> His glory fills the whole earth.
> The foundations of the doorways shook at the sound of
> their voices, and the temple was filled with smoke.
> Then I said:
> Woe is me, for I am ruined,
> because I am a man
> of unclean lips and live among a people
> of unclean lips, and because my eyes have seen the
> King, the LORD of Hosts.
> Then one of the seraphim flew to me, and in his hand
> was a glowing coal that he had taken from the altar with
> tongs. He touched my mouth with it and said:
> Now that this has touched your lips,
> your wickedness is removed,
> and your sin is atoned for. (Isa. 6:1–7)

This is indeed the correct view of God. He alone is high and lifted up. He alone is worthy, and the whole earth is filled with His glory—even when it doesn't look that way to us. That is who God is, no matter what circumstances we may face. Unclean—apart from the grace of God in Jesus Christ—that is who we are. When we understand exactly what God accomplished for us when Jesus paid the price of our sin, worship is our only reasonable response. And as we worship, we can expect His presence.

Grace—Our Only Hope

No matter how holy or righteous we may think we are, we are not worthy of God's presence in our own power and strength. The only hope we have is that mercy will descend from God's throne and, by grace, touch our "unclean lips." Only then will we be able to stand in God's presence and present our sacrifice of praise.

I've always loved the music and ministry of Steven Curtis Chapman. I admired his song writing and his skill as a guitarist and singer. I identified with so many of his songs and loved to play and sing his music. There's no doubt he had a great influence on me as a songwriter.

One time I was visiting another early influence in my songwriting ministry, Brent Lamb. Brent was the first artist to record one of my songs and was a great encouragement to me. I was at Brent's house when the doorbell rang. He asked me to answer the door and when I did, there he was—Steven Curtis Chapman, mullet and all! Brent knew how much I admired Steven Curtis, and being a close friend of his, he called and asked him to come by to meet me. I was blown away. We spent the afternoon playing football and watching *The Hunt for Red October*. I enjoyed seeing the real side of this man who had influenced my music so much.

It's not likely I would have ever met Steven Curtis without Brent Lamb. And it is certain I would have never known God without the sacrifice of Jesus Christ. I would have never earned His favor or merited an audience with Him. I needed a mediator—someone who could make a way. God provided one—His name is Jesus.

The Father we worship is the same God Abraham worshipped. He is the One who provided the lamb of sacrifice on Mount Moriah. He is the same God who met with Jacob and the same God who revealed Himself to Moses and delivered the Israelites from slavery. He is the same God who chose Mary and Joseph, and the One the apostle Paul honored, worshipped, and served.

As we have seen, Jesus is the express image of God. He is the incarnation of Truth, and thus anything that contradicts who He is (His character) or what He has said is not truth.

Love came down to us in Jesus. We didn't deserve that kind of grace. We are indeed recipients of God's unmerited favor—grace that is unending and everlasting. God's grace is not dependent upon ritual or tradition, performance or precision. It is always dependent, however, upon our submission to the Truth; Jesus is the revelation of who God really is. As we believe in the revelation of God, we receive the gift of God's grace, which is everlasting life:

> *"For God so loved the world that He gave His only begotten Son, that whoever believes in Him should not perish but have everlasting life. For God did not send His Son into the world to condemn the world, but that the world through Him might be saved. He who believes in Him is not condemned; but he who does not believe is condemned already, because he has not believed in the name of the only begotten Son of God."* (John 3:16–18 NKJV)

How do you "see" God? Is He a loving Father? A friend? Consider the times and ways you have "seen" God in your own life.

Father	Healer
Your Peace	Your Righteousness
Lord/Master	Protector
Savior/Redeemer	Provider
Counselor	Comforter
Friend	Sustainer

Isaiah may have "seen" God as all of these things, but first and foremost he "saw" his position—and ours—relative to God! Apart from a Savior, we are unworthy and unable to stand in God's glorious presence.

How do you "see" yourself?

Sinner	Forgiven
Worthless	Worthy
Forgotten/Overlooked	Chosen (from foundation of earth)
Unwanted	Adopted
Condemned	Pardoned

Call to Worship

Grace! That determines how God "sees" His children. Without grace, we could never worship God. Entering His presence would surely condemn us to death. But, praise His holy name, His grace is sufficient! God so loved the world that He gave and He gave and He gave . . . and He continues to give today. Let us worship the Father in spirit and in truth, for He is worthy!

Reflections

- True worship requires that we understand God's supremacy and our inadequacy in light of His greatness.
- God alone is able to cleanse us by His grace and make us worthy of His glorious presence.
- Without grace we could never worship God; entering His presence would surely condemn us to death.
- God's grace came down to us in Jesus—undeserved, unmerited grace.

Prayer

Dear Lord, thank You for Your grace; grace that could see beyond my failure and love me as I was; grace that would pay the ultimate price so that I might know love. Amen.

LOVE

Song of Worship

"Life and Breath"

Jesus, Master and Creator, Counselor and Savior
How marvelous You are
As I come into Your presence With honor and in reverence
I give You all my heart

Jesus King of kings forever Heaven's priceless treasure
A living sacrifice
I stand humbled by Your mercy ever undeserving
Of eternal life

(Chorus)
You are the way, You are the truth, You are alive in me
Jesus You are Life and breath to me
So with all of my heart, all of my mind, all of my strength
I will honor You Lord
Jesus You are Life and breath to me

16

Love Came Down

Each of us was **created** by God for
relationship with Him, but we can only enjoy
that relationship by God's **grace**.
God's great **love** for us [is] demonstrated
in Christ Jesus.

*The full and perfect expression of God's great love
for us is His Son, Jesus Christ.*

We have read that the Creator of all things, who made us to worship Him in spirit and in truth, chose to come to Earth, take on human form with all its frailties and limitations, and make a way for us by grace to be worthy of His presence. What could motivate God to do such a thing? The only answer is love.

*[Jesus], existing in the form of God, did not consider equality
with God as something to be used for His own advantage.
Instead He emptied Himself by assuming the form of a slave,*

taking on the likeness of men. And when He had come as a
man in His external form, He humbled Himself by becoming
obedient to the point of death—even to death on a cross.
(Phil. 2:6–8)

God Is Love

God *is* love. God always has been and always will be love, for God
never changes.

God is love, and the one who remains in love remains in God,
and God remains in him. (1 John 4:16)

Expressing His love for us is so important to God that He was
willing to send Himself in human form to die in order to demonstrate
real love. And Jesus calls us to demonstrate this same kind of love for
others:

"No one has greater love than this, that someone would lay
down his life for his friends. You are My friends if you do what
I command you." (John 15:13–14)

There is a beautiful story that a friend once told me. As the story
begins, it was a bitterly cold day in northern France. World War II was
headed to its conclusion, but there were still many days of fighting
ahead. Two soldiers—I'll call them Corporal Bill Sanders and Private
Joel Anderson—sat in a foxhole and heard the bad news—there was a
mission that had to be carried out, and Bill had been chosen to go. The
platoon leader made it clear: this mission was likely to cost Bill his life,
but freedom for thousands was dependent on his act of courage.

Joel was very familiar with Bill's life story—after all, he had spent
weeks trudging through the mud with Bill, bringing liberty to a people
ravaged by war. Joel had listened for hours as Bill had read the letters
from his wife and three young children back home. He loved hearing
the stories about their life together.

Joel had somehow been "grafted into Bill's family" during those
many hours together. Joel knew that Bill had a good reason to live—his
wife and kids needed him desperately. But the mission to liberate people
fighting for their families there in France was essential.

Joel *knew* what he had to do. He had a deep sense that just maybe
he had been born for such a time as this—the love he held for Bill and

his family was overwhelming. Joel convinced the platoon leader to send him on this deadly mission instead of Bill.

Joel laid down his life that day for his friend. His sacrifice not only impacted the war effort, but also countless lives in his rural hometown for generations to come. Bill returned home to his family and spent the rest of his life telling the story of how Joel had chosen to lay down his life that day for his friend. And through Bill's efforts, Joel's heroism has impacted millions around the world.

God's Love Cost Him Dearly

That story paints a perfect picture of real, sacrificial love in action. In the same manner, Jesus laid down His precious life for me—and for you. Jesus chose to pay the price for all our sins at Calvary. He is the Lamb of God who experienced the pain of a real flesh-and-blood death in our place. That's how much God loves us. Love is who He is, and His love for us cost Him dearly. How could we not want to tell the world about this wonderful Friend and Savior?

Every day people "lay down their lives" for others. Maybe one or more of these actions are demonstrated through your life or someone you know:

- Sacrificial giving to those in need (money and/or material things)
- Investing time in the lives of others
- Giving up self-interests for the interests of others
- Caring for others' needs (physical, emotional, mental, or spiritual)
- Praying/interceding for others consistently
- Providing a financial inheritance
- Working hard to provide for family
- Serving in the military to ensure freedom
- Being willing to donate organs so that others may live—or live better lives

Call to Worship

All of these activities are evidence of love. Because love must express itself through actions, there is *always* evidence of real love. Perhaps you can think of some of the evidences of God's love for *you*. Many things could come to your mind, but the greatest evidence of God's love for each of us is the life, death, and resurrection of Jesus Christ. Such self-less love requires our response of worship.

Reflections

- God is love and will always be true to His nature.
- God chose to reveal His great love for us through the life, death, and resurrection of Jesus.
- There is no greater expression of love than laying down one's life for another. Jesus laid down His life for each of us.
- We should want to tell others about God's incredible love.

Prayer

Heavenly Father, thank You for Jesus who came to earth, lived a perfect life, sacrificed Himself for my sin, and rose again to reign forever. Without Christ I would never have known You or be welcomed into Your presence. Thank You for my Savior. Amen.

17

Worship: Our Response to God's Great Love

God's love elicits a response of love from us—worship!

We've seen that God's grace is a direct result of His love for His people. There is no other explanation for an omnipotent, all-powerful God who chooses to overwhelm our human limitations and make a way for us to know Him and receive His promises. The Bible shows us that God always has been and always will be love. It is His nature, His expression, His identity; and as we have learned, God will always be consistently true to Himself. No matter how bleak our circumstances may look, nothing can ever separate us from God's love:

> *Who can separate us from the love of Christ? Can affliction or anguish or persecution or famine or nakedness or danger or sword? . . . For I am persuaded that neither death nor life, nor angels nor rulers, nor things present, nor things to come, nor powers, nor height, nor depth, nor any other created thing will have the power to separate us from the love of God that is in Christ Jesus our Lord! (Rom. 8:35, 38–39)*

So, love is not only a good idea; it is the essence of God. And God expects His overwhelming love for us to elicit a response of love from us— worship! How could we not worship the One who loves us this much?

Throughout Scripture, whenever God's people recognized that God's grace, motivated by His incredible love, had intervened in their lives, they were quick to worship Him. Let's take a look at the biblical accounts of two very different individuals who experienced God's love and grace and responded with worship—Nehemiah and Mary, the mother of Jesus.

Nehemiah's Story

The story of Nehemiah is a classic example of what it means to experience God. Nehemiah's account walks us through every one of the seven realities in the process of experiencing God outlined by Blackaby and King in *Experiencing God*—and worship was his response!

The task of rebuilding the walls was indeed a God-sized assignment that could be completed only by God's grace. Simply asking the king for permission was a major step of faith for Nehemiah. As we have seen, faith and action are always required as we respond to God's invitation to join Him as He works. Nehemiah said to the king,

> *"If it pleases the king, and if your servant has found favor with you, send me to Judah and to the city where my ancestors are buried, so that I may rebuild it." (Neh. 2:5)*

The king gave his approval, but Nehemiah had to make many major adjustments in his life and persevere through great opposition to join God in this mighty kingdom endeavor. And when the walls were finished, Nehemiah led God's people in one of the great corporate worship moments in Scripture:

> *I brought the leaders of Judah up on top of the wall, and I appointed two large processions that gave thanks. . . . The singers sang, with Jezrahiah as the leader. On that day they offered great sacrifices and rejoiced because God had given them great joy. The women and children also celebrated, and Jerusalem's rejoicing was heard far away. (Neh. 12:31, 42–43)*

Nehemiah's story was personal and yet very public. It took great faith and corresponding action by all of God's people to respond to God's invitation through Nehemiah's leadership. The result was that *the people experienced God* as the walls were rebuilt. Their obedience to God led to one of the greatest corporate worship events in the history of the world!

Read More about It

- Petitioning the king: Nehemiah 2:1–8
- Making preparations: Nehemiah 2:11–20
- The work begins: Nehemiah 3:1–32
- Hostile plots are thwarted: Nehemiah 4:1–23
- Dealing with complaints: Nehemiah 5:1–13
- Outsmarting the enemy: Nehemiah 6:1–14
- The wall is completed: Nehemiah 6:15–19
- The exiles return: Nehemiah 7:5–73
- The people worship: Nehemiah 8:1–18

Mary's Story

Unlike Nehemiah's story, Mary's story is very personal and mostly private. As she embraced being chosen by God to become the mother of the Savior of the world, Mary's life was changed forever. Surely Mary had her own "crisis of belief" as she responded to God's invitation to join Him as He worked, and God responded to her need. She still endured doubt, hardship, scorn, and ridicule along the way to her destiny. But Mary experienced God in the process in ways no one could possibly imagine.

After submitting to God's will for her life, Mary traveled to be with her relative Elizabeth, and she discovered that Elizabeth also was pregnant with a son. As soon as Mary reached Elizabeth's house, God made clear that He was indeed present with her:

> In those days Mary set out and hurried to a town in the hill country of Judah where she entered Zechariah's house and greeted Elizabeth. When Elizabeth heard Mary's greeting, the baby leaped inside her, and Elizabeth was filled with the Holy Spirit. Then she exclaimed with a loud cry:
> You are the most blessed of women, and your child will be blessed! (Luke 1:39–42)

Mary's response to God's gracious affirmation through Elizabeth was worship:

> *"My soul proclaims the greatness of the Lord, and my spirit has rejoiced in God my Savior, because He has looked with favor on the humble condition of His slave. Surely, from now on all generations will call me blessed, because the Mighty One has done great things for me, and His name is holy."* (Luke 1:46–49)

Read More about It

- An angel appears to Mary: Luke 1:26–38
- Mary visits Elizabeth: Luke 1:39–45
- Mary's song of praise: Luke 1:46–55

Spontaneous Worship

The stories of Mary and Nehemiah give us two very different but clear examples of God's people responding to His loving intervention in their lives. When we recognize what God has done for us, and the love that motivates His actions, our worship becomes more spontaneous. Worship is both a natural human response and a spiritual reaction to who God is and what He has done.

My friend and coauthor, Stan Moser, encountered a young woman at church who provides a great modern-day example of worship in response to what God has done. Here is the story in his words:

> At a recent Wednesday night service, my wife, Sue, pointed out a young lady named Deborah just before the service began. When Sue met this young woman last year, Deborah was using a walker and could barely even stand. She was stricken with multiple sclerosis, and she had been told that her only alternative was to go to the nursing home to live out what was left of her life.
>
> But Deborah had a revelation—a revelation that defied logic. Deborah was convinced that she had a Redeemer, One whose name is more powerful than multiple sclerosis—One who

loves her enough to die for her and make it possible for her to overcome the adversary who wants to destroy her life. His name is Jesus—the name above all names.

When Sue first met Deborah, she felt led to go to the altar and pray for her. Deborah needed a miracle, and God was ready to meet her need! Sue responded to God's invitation to join Him with Deborah at the altar. There was no visible change that night, but God was definitely working.

Now, one year later, I watched across the auditorium as Deborah began to worship God with all her heart, all her soul, and all her strength. The worship team started with a Reuben Morgan song, "My Redeemer Lives." We all worshipped, but Deborah *worshipped!*

She wasn't in a wheelchair, and she no longer used a walker. This vibrant, joy-filled woman was standing and exalting her God with uplifted hands and a grateful heart. I was moved to tears as I watched this beloved daughter of Almighty God respond to the revelation of who God is and what God had done in her life!

And then it struck me: I should be worshipping the same way. *My* Redeemer lives as well! He is the One who redeemed my life from the fiery pit; the One who cast my sin into a sea of forgetfulness; the Lamb who loved me enough to die, face all the forces the adversary could muster, and return to earth victorious over sin and death.

Now that's what I call revelation—who He is and what He has done! It's true: *My* Redeemer lives! *Your* Redeemer lives! You may not have overcome a life-threatening disease like Deborah, but you most definitely have been delivered from a death sentence of sin. He *is* Savior, Deliverer, Prince of Peace, Almighty God—the Name above all names. We have every reason to respond to the great love God has expressed and experience Him in worship!

Call to Worship

God has revealed Himself to us as our Savior, Friend, Counselor, Redeemer, and so much more. Cry out to God for answers to even the most difficult issues you are facing. Recall who He is and what He has done in your life. God has promised to meet you as you worship, and He will!

Reflections

- God's grace is a direct result of His love for His people.
- God's very nature is love, and nothing can ever separate us from His love.
- God expects His overwhelming love for us to elicit a response of love from us—worship!
- God invited Nehemiah and Mary to join Him as He worked, and they responded with faith and action. As a result, they experienced God and worshipped Him in response.
- When we recognize the love God has for us and what He has done for us, our natural response is to worship Him.
- Worship should *always* be our response to God's revelation!

Prayer

Dear God, You have loved me with a perfect love.
Let my life be lived as an expression of my gratitude
for all You have done for me. My Redeemer lives! Amen.

18

Love One Another

God's love for us empowers us to love one another.

Our love for God in response to His love for us is only step one for believers. God has also called us to love one another:

> [Jesus] answered: "Love the Lord your God with all your heart, with all your soul, with all your strength, and with all your mind; and your neighbor as yourself." (Luke 10:27)

> "I give you a new commandment: love one another. Just as I have loved you, you must also love one another. By this all people will know that you are My disciples, if you have love for one another." (John 13:34–35)

Our response to God's great love must be reflected not only in our attitudes and actions toward God, but also in our attitudes and actions toward those around us. As we honor God's instruction, our worship is unhindered.

A Biblical Picture of Love

As we have seen, the Bible tells us that God is love. The Bible also tells us that we were created in God's image: "God said, 'Let Us make man in Our image, according to Our likeness'" (Gen. 1:26). Furthermore, we know that God doesn't love us in word only, but also in deed: "God proves His own love for us in that while we were still sinners Christ died for us" (Rom. 5:8).

Therefore, as we embrace the grace-filled life that God provides, love must flow through our words and our actions toward one another. As this verse from 1 John tells us, "We love because He first loved us" (4:19). So, we are both commanded and qualified to love God and one another.

Paul's words to the Colossian church show us how love for one another should look:

> Therefore, God's chosen ones, holy and loved, put on heart-felt compassion, kindness, humility, gentleness, and patience, accepting one another and forgiving one another if anyone has a complaint against another. Just as the Lord has forgiven you, so also you must forgive. Above all, put on love—the perfect bond of unity. And let the peace of the Messiah, to which you were also called in one body, control your hearts. Be thankful. (Col. 3:12–15)

Can you see the picture of love here? We are the elect of God, which means that God chose us. And He has chosen to dwell in us and among us. We are holy because He is holy, and that allows us to approach His throne of grace without any hindrance or obstacles. He loved us enough to die for us, and that love must set the tone for our relationships with one another.

Our attitude and actions toward one another must be tender, merciful, kind, humble, meek, longsuffering, and forgiving. With love—the bond of perfection—in place, the Word of God will flow through us to one another, and peace and thanksgiving will abound—as well as praise!

Love Overflowing

With our attitude and actions toward one another in right order, we can gather corporately with expectation. As we lift our voices to the

Lord in worship, with grace in our hearts, the love we have for God will overflow to those around us; and their lives will be changed forever.

Some years ago when I was serving as a church worship leader in Carrollton, Texas, I witnessed the love of God pour out of the body of Christ on my dear friends, Mark and Marilyn Nesbit. Their daughter, Meredith, a freshman in college at the time, was tragically killed in an automobile accident while returning home from school for the Thanksgiving holiday.

As you can imagine, the entire church, and our worship team in particular, rallied around this grief-stricken family. Mark and Marilyn were devastated, but even in their broken place, they worshipped; and they called us all to a higher place of worship, as well.

As we gathered for the memorial service, there were many testimonials and tears. Mark and Marilyn didn't ask for tears and sorrow that day, although we all shared their grief. But they did ask that I lead the congregation in intimate worship of our great God and Savior! They wanted us to worship God and to invite His glorious presence even in the midst of their tragedy.

I remember clutching my guitar close to my chest and begging God for the grace to honor their deepest desire—and He responded. We sang Meredith's favorite song that day, "Run to the Cross," with all the joy and strength we could muster.

Run to the cross, run to the cross
There you will find God's love divine, run to the cross
That blood-stained place of love and grace
God now awaits, run to the cross.[1]

Jesus' sacrifice on the cross at Calvary had already bridged the great divide for Meredith, and we wept, worshipped, and celebrated her victory—all at the same time.

Our singing and worship that day transcended the moment of tragedy and led our entire church forward with renewed hope and confidence that our Redeemer lives and cares about each one of us. As we lifted our voices in praise to our God, barriers were broken down that day—barriers that separated us from God and barriers that separated men and women in our fellowship from one another. Love Himself broke through that day as we all ran to the cross together. I later took a print copy of the song and framed it for Mark and Marilyn. On the cover I signed it "For Meredith." Sometime later I saw it displayed in their home and remembered that powerful day of worship.

The question Paul asks in 1 Corinthians 15:55 came to mind. "O Death, where is your victory? O Death, where is your sting?" Even in the face of death, the enemy's ultimate weapon, our God wins the day and remains worthy of our worship.

According to Jesus' own words, what will allow those around us to know that we are His? Will going to church, giving to those in need, worshipping, or praying? All of our activities are good and necessary, but Jesus made it clear that unless we reach out to one another in love, the world will not recognize that we are His disciples. As the following passage from 1 John affirms, love is the very thing that indicates we are born of God:

> Dear friends, let us love one another, because love is from God, and everyone who loves has been born of God and knows God. The one who does not love does not know God, because God is love. (4:7–8)

If we know and love God, love should flow freely in our lives. In fact, without love, our good deeds and our spiritual gifts are ineffective.

> If I speak the languages of men and of angels, but do not have love, I am a sounding gong or a clanging cymbal. If I have the gift of prophecy, and understand all mysteries and all knowledge, and if I have all faith, so that I can move mountains, but do not have love, I am nothing. And if I donate all my goods to feed the poor, and if I give my body to be burned, but do not have love, I gain nothing. (1 Cor. 13:1–3)

In addition to instructing us to love one another, Jesus declared that we are to be "salt and light" to the world around us. He has chosen to dwell in each of us through the Holy Spirit and to reach the unsaved through us. The key is always found in abiding in Christ and allowing His Spirit to work through us.

> "You are the salt of the earth. But if the salt should lose its taste, how can it be made salty? . . . You are the light of the world . . . Let your light shine before men, so that they may see your good works and give glory to your Father in heaven." (Matt. 5:13–14, 16)

> "I am the vine; you are the branches. The one who remains in Me and I in him produces much fruit, because you can do nothing without Me." (John 15:5)

Call to Worship

God is love, and God wants to express His love through us—the body of Christ—to believers and to the unsaved. God always initiates, and we simply respond. As we grasp the width, depth, and breadth of His love for us, our worship will express and demonstrate love in return.

Reflections

- We love because God first loved us.
- God's love for us requires that we love one another.
- When our attitudes and actions toward one another are in right order, we may worship corporately with expectation.
- Love flows through our worship to touch the lives of others.
- The world recognizes that we are His by the way we love one another.
- All we do is done in vain unless we are motivated by love.
- Loving one another is not a request; it is God's command.

Prayer

Almighty God, You have taught me to love and modeled love for me. Forgive me for the sin of selfishness in my life. Help me show the world I belong to You by the love I give to those around me. Amen.

Notes

1. "Run to the Cross" written by Mike Harland, ©1999 Centergetic Music (ASCAP). All Rights Reserved. Used by Permission. International Copyright Secured.

19

The Passageway
to the Heart

God calls us to love others by sharing His Word.

As we have seen, we are commanded to love others, and one of the best ways we love others is to share God's Word with them. As we speak or sing the Word of God, we, as well as others around us, hear that Word proclaimed. And as each of us hears the Word, faith begins to rise in our hearts:

> *So then faith comes by hearing, and hearing by the word of God. (Rom. 10:17 NKJV)*

The ear really is the passageway to the heart. As we speak words of faith and grace to one another, the faith that is birthed and nurtured in our hearts overflows to those around us. Then we begin to speak that word that has been planted by grace in our hearts.

It is true: what is in our hearts determines what comes out of our mouths.

"For the mouth speaks from the overflow of the heart. A good man produces good things from his storeroom of good, and an evil man produces evil things from his storeroom of evil." (Matt. 12:34–35)

It is up to all of us to see that our hearts are filled with words of faith, hope, and love! One of the best ways to fill our hearts with words of faith, hope, and love is to worship. Our worship expression makes a difference in our own lives and in the lives of those we encounter every day.

Filling Our Hearts in Worship

Carefully consider the following three statements about worship. They are essential to understanding what happens as we fill our hearts in worship, receiving the power available to us as we worship the King of kings!

1. *Worship is directional.* When we speak or sing words of grace, thanksgiving, and praise to the King of kings, those around us hear those words; and the cycle of faith that comes by hearing repeats. Speaking to one another with psalms, hymns, and spiritual songs— filling our homes and churches with worship and worship music— reinforces God's Word and edifies everyone around us. The effect of worship flows *upward* to God and *outward* to fellow believers. And God will always respond!

2. *Worship is motivational.* Worship invites the presence of the Lord, and when we encounter Him, we are *motivated* to accept His invitation to join Him as He works. When God's people worship in spirit and truth, there is no need to convince them to step into ministry opportunities. Worship motivates us to witness, give, and serve as we receive more revelation of God's greatness in our lives. I have attended many conferences and training events in my life and I have plenty of guilt to show for it. But when I have encountered Christ, the motivation to witness, to serve, to give, happens naturally. No amount of "ought to" compares with the power of "want to." And "want to" only comes from being with Christ.

Even those who don't believe or lack real commitment to God are motivated by worship. The story of the woman at the well from John 4 is a great example. She found herself in the presence of God Himself, and that revelation led her to bring the entire village out to hear from

Jesus. Her response to Jesus introduced an entire community to the Savior of the world, and many believed!

> *Now many Samaritans from that town believed in Him*
> *because of what the woman said when she testified.*
> *(John 4:39)*

3. *Worship is continual.* Around the very throne of God, there is a *continual*—never-ending—proclamation of praise and adoration for the Holy One. I love the picture of worship in heaven provided in the book of Revelation:

> *Each of the four living creatures had six wings; they were*
> *covered with eyes around and inside. Day and night they*
> *never stop, saying:*
> *Holy, holy, holy,*
> *Lord God, the Almighty,*
> *who was, who is, and who is coming.*
> *Whenever the living creatures give glory, honor, and*
> *thanks to the One seated on the throne, the One who lives*
> *forever and ever, the 24 elders fall down before the One*
> *seated on the throne, [and] worship the One who lives*
> *forever and ever. (Rev. 4:8–10)*

The Hebrew word *shachach*, which is used more than one hundred times in the Old Testament alone, indicates a physical response of bowing and stooping in order to show reverence for the One who was and is greater than all others. That's what is transpiring over and over again around the throne of God right now!

Celestial beings are repeatedly bowing before the throne of God, crying, "Holy, holy, holy, Lord God, the Almighty, who was, who is, and who is coming!" (Rev. 4:8). Perhaps the constant repetition is not habit but is due to an ever-increasing revelation of God's greatness, which occurs every time they rise and look into His glorious countenance. They *continually* worship at the very throne of God Almighty. And forever, every time they bow and cry holy, they rise again to encounter further revelation of the One who was and is and is to come.

There is no shortage of revelation or any lingering doubts about the love of God in heaven. God is present in all His glory, and His love for His people cannot be denied. Perhaps this is why worship continues night and day in heaven! Likewise, as we worship God in spirit and truth on Earth, Truth Himself penetrates our hearts, reveals Himself, and elicits a response that, in turn, increases our expression of worship. God is love, and worship will *always* be our response to God's revelation—now and forever!

Our focus during times of corporate worship must be on God Himself. Yet there are many distractions that can keep us from truly entering into worship. Think of some ways you have been motivated to enter into corporate worship.

- Seeing others sing/worship
- Being encouraged by the pastor or worship leader to worship
- Seeing others worship with enthusiasm, excitement, or heartfelt emotion (e.g., lifting hands, shouting praises, bowing reverently)
- Hearing the music crescendo
- Watching a baptism
- Singing your favorite songs
- Celebrating special holidays such as Christmas and Easter
- Praying

Call to Worship

In addition to times of corporate worship, we can continue to worship throughout our daily routine. Consider these times when worship is possible.

- While driving to and from appointments
- While cleaning the house or doing other chores
- While exercising
- When gathering as a family for meals and other activities
- While getting dressed in the morning
- While getting ready for bed

When worship becomes a focus every day, it's not really difficult to find time. God truly loves to hear our voice of praise and adoration. And as our revelation of His great love for us grows, worship is our never-ending response—throughout all of eternity!

Reflections

- We are commanded to love one another and share God's Word with those around us.

- Faith comes by hearing the Word of God.
- The ear is the passageway to the heart, and our words reveal what is in our hearts.
- As God's Word penetrates our hearts, our words will build faith in those around us.
- Worship is directional: it flows upward to God but outwardly impacts our fellow believers.
- Worship is motivational: it motivates us to witness, give, and serve as we receive more revelation of God's greatness in our lives.
- Worship is continual: it elicits a response that, in turn, increases our expression of worship.

Prayer

Jesus, thank You for loving me and for working in my life. Let my service grow out of my worship of You instead of trying to earn Your love with my service. Show me the difference. Amen.

20

Let Worship Begin Here and Now!

God wants us to allow His love to flow through us.

Throughout this section we have examined a biblical picture of the great love that God has for us—love that is unmerited and requires us to love one another. The very act of loving one another is an expression of worship. Let's examine just what love is and what we can expect love to do.

The Greatest Expression of God's Love

As we have seen, our worship begins with love—God's love for us and our love for God. He alone is worthy. He is the One who took the initiative. He created us for worship and loved us enough to make a way for us to enter His presence. God loved the world so much that He sent His only son, Jesus.

Jesus Christ is the greatest expression of God's love for us. He paid the price for all our shortcomings and made a way for us to experience the presence of God. He has become the living sacrifice that defines true love. God's expression of love in sending Jesus to redeem mankind compels us to honor His command to love one another:

> For Christ's love compels us, since we have reached this conclusion: if One died for all, then all died. And He died for all so that those who live should no longer live for themselves, but for the One who died for them and was raised. (2 Cor. 5:14–15)

Once we receive a clear revelation of God's love through the sacrifice of Jesus for our sins, worship becomes our expression of love for God in return.

Jesus said, "Love one another as I have loved you" (John 15:12). The only way to fulfill that command is to allow the love of God to flow through us to others. Jesus is the One who laid down His very life for us, and for those around us. And He has chosen to dwell in us and express His great love for mankind through us.

What Love Is and What Love Isn't

> Love is patient; love is kind. Love does not envy; is not boastful; is not conceited; does not act improperly; is not selfish; is not provoked; does not keep a record of wrongs; finds no joy in unrighteousness, but rejoices in the truth; bears all things, believes all things, hopes all things, endures all things. (1 Cor. 13:4–7)

If you have been in church very long, you have undoubtedly read this wonderful passage about love. The description is clear, and the attributes of love are so admirable. Of course, love is like faith—we can believe in love, have love, be loved, and understand love, but without corresponding action, our love simply doesn't fulfill its purpose.

One of my favorite movies is *The Princess Bride*. In this wonderful film, a young lady named Buttercup encounters Westley (a.k.a. Farmboy) in the stable. The chemistry between the two is immediate, and ultimately she discovers that Westley is her "one true love." As the evil Prince Humperdink, who wants Buttercup for his bride, attempts to kill Westley, the story unfolds.

At one point the Prince captures and tortures Westley; and frankly, he looks pretty dead to me. His compatriot, a giant named Fezzik, drags Westley's body to Miracle Max, played by Billy Crystal—for a miracle—of course! Fezzik places Westley's body very carefully on the table. Then Miracle Max picks up Westley's limp arm and drops it with a loud and immediate thud.

Max shouts, "What do you want from me? I'm retired!" But when pressed to look again, with the promise of undermining Humperdink, the miracle man declares, "He's not *all* dead, he's just *mostly* dead."

Sometimes that phrase describes the love we express as the body of Christ. Often after being pursued by God, we figure it out and accept Jesus, our one true love. But the love that flows from us to others is, well, *mostly* dead. And that is understandable. After all, people can be pretty mean sometimes, and many of us seem to have issues from childhood, and . . . shall I go on? In our hearts, we want to show the love of Christ to everyone, but we have limitations that seem to bind us against our will.

What Love Does

The Bible gives us the answer to this dilemma, which results in genuine true love—love for one another. And *that* kind of love never fails.

> Love never ends. . . . Now these three remain: faith, hope, and love. But the greatest of these is love. (1 Cor. 13:8, 13)

What is the answer? Take a look at Paul's letter to the Ephesians:

> Therefore, be imitators of God, as dearly loved children. And walk in love, as the Messiah also loved us and gave Himself for us, a sacrificial and fragrant offering to God. (Eph. 5:1–2)

The answer to bringing our "*mostly* dead" love back to life is found in an ever-increasing revelation of our "*completely* alive" Savior and His great love for us! We have been given so much—so much evidence of Love. Once we really do understand who He is and what He has done, it is possible to pour out long-suffering love; envy-free love; kind love; bearing, believing, hoping, and enduring love on others around us.

Ultimately Westley comes back to life and rescues Buttercup from the prince in the nick of time; and they live happily ever after. Ultimately we will understand that this is exactly what God has done for us in Jesus Christ. Our One True Love came and found us. He rescued us from a life of doom, and He never, ever gives up. True love is this: that a man lay down his life for another.

A personal experience with that kind of love happened for me when my wife and I began to face the realities of her breast cancer. I look back on it now and realize I had so much growing up to do! God used the experience to cause growth to happen. I remember the morning after her biopsy like it was yesterday. It was a Saturday and I sat in my recliner almost in a blind stare for a long time. I had this incredible thought over and over: *I would give anything to trade places with her. Why can't it be me? Why does she have to go through this?* That love would be the reason I would gladly attend to her for the weeks ahead. I didn't serve her out of obligation. It was the natural response of love. It's not that I'm so noble. It's that love is just that strong. My love for her made me want to take her burden and make it my own.

Call to Worship

No one has ever modeled selfless love like Jesus. Romans 5:8 reminds us that His love, and not our worth, sent Jesus to the cross. As we allow God's love for us to flow through us without hesitation and limitation, we are responding to God's revelation of who He is and what He has done. Love, Himself, compels us to worship. Let us put our response of love into action toward God and one another—every day.

Reflections

- Worship begins with love—God's love for us and our love for God.
- God is love, and His greatest expression of love for us is Jesus Christ.
- God desires us to allow His love to flow through us to others.
- Our faith must be expressed through love—love for God and love for others.

Prayer

Heavenly Father, thank You for loving me when I was a sinner and separated from You. Teach me how to love even when love is not deserved. Amen.

RESPONSE

Song of Worship

"The Stand"

You stood before creation
Eternity in Your hand
You spoke the earth into motion
My soul now to stand

You stood before my failure
And carried the cross for my shame
My sin weighed upon Your shoulders
My soul now to stand

So what could I say?
And what could I do?
But offer this heart Oh God
Completely to You

(Chorus)
I'll stand my stand
With arms high and heart abandoned
In awe of the one who gave it all
I'll stand my stand

WORDS AND MUSIC BY JOEL HOUSTON
©2005 JOEL HOUSTON/HILLSONG PUBLISHING
(ADM. IN THE US & CANADA BY INTEGRITY'S HOSANNA! MUSIC)/ASCAP
C/O INTEGRITY MEDIA, INC., 1000 CODY ROAD, MOBILE, AL 36695

21

Our Response: Service and Surrender

Each of us was **created** by God for relationship with Him, but we can only enjoy that relationship by God's **grace**. God's great **love** for us, demonstrated in Christ Jesus, initiates our **response**.

Responding to God's revelation in a manner that is pleasing to Him involves service and surrender.

As we have seen so far, God is love and His grace abounds toward us every day. Through Jesus Christ, the sacrificial Lamb of God, we are able to enter God's glorious presence and receive from the very throne of grace. What's more, God continues to reveal Himself and His efforts on our behalf every day.

It is up to us to respond and worship God for who He is and what He has done. But what should that response look like? How can we respond to God's revelation in a manner that is pleasing to Him?

Service: Love in Action

God's love for us is thorough and everlasting. In expressing His love for us through the sacrifice of His beloved Son, Jesus, God was being true to His nature:

> "For God loved the world in this way: He gave His One and Only Son." (John 3:16)

God is love, and God made us in His image. Our response to God's love should be to love in return—to love God and to love one another. We love because He first loved us, for all things begin in Him:

> For from Him and through Him and to Him are all things. [For all things originate with Him and come from Him; all things live through Him, and all things center in and tend to consummate and to end in Him.] To Him be glory forever! Amen (so be it). (Rom. 11:36 AMP)

Still, we must *respond*—we must put our love into action! Love without action is similar to faith without works—it's dead. Our love should look like the love we read about in 1 Corinthians 13, and it should result in service and good deeds, as these verses from the book of 1 John further explain:

> This is how we have come to know love: He laid down His life for us. We should also lay down our lives for our brothers. If anyone has this world's goods and sees his brother in need but shuts off his compassion from him—how can God's love reside in him?
> Little children, we must not love in word or speech, but in deed and truth; that is how we will know we are of the truth, and will convince our hearts in His presence. (1 John 3:16–19)

Complete Surrender

Jesus gave us the ultimate example of surrendering to the plans and purposes of God. He really did choose to walk the road to Calvary and take the weight of our sins upon His guiltless body. God mercifully sacrificed real, unblemished flesh and blood in order to make a way for us to enter His presence. Jesus, the Lamb of God, paid the complete and total price for our freedom, and our response of worship is likewise costly:

> I APPEAL to you therefore, brethren, and beg of you in view of [all] the mercies of God, to make a decisive dedication of your bodies [presenting all your members and faculties] as a **living sacrifice**, holy (devoted, consecrated) and well pleasing to God, which is your reasonable (rational, intelligent) service and spiritual worship. (Rom. 12:1 AMP, emphasis added)

Our response to God's love must be to express love, which requires action. We are to serve others in tangible ways. Even so, our words and actions are not enough. Our tithes and offerings are not enough. There is only one thing that makes our service appropriate and sufficient: complete surrender.

Totally surrendering our hearts and our lives to God—that is our reasonable, rational, intelligent response. Responding to God in this way requires surrender in every area of our lives—laying down our desires (if they are different from God's) and taking up God's desires moment by moment of every day.

Our lives really *can* become a living sacrifice—often in the most practical ways. Many times what we see as sacrifice is really God's way of moving us toward our destiny. I was confronted with that truth as a college student.

Sacrifice Is a Choice

Sports are important to most young boys and girls. Whether they are good at a particular sport isn't always the issue. Just being on the team—being included and having an identity—is a big deal, particularly in the teenage years.

I grew up playing baseball *and* playing guitar. And frankly, I loved both activities. I guess I was born for a stage of some kind! I'm pretty sure I was great at both baseball and music . . . well, at least my mom and dad thought I was.

When I was a sophomore at Delta State University in Cleveland, Mississippi, my baseball career was in full bloom—and so was my music ministry. Until that year both interests had coincided very well, but that was about to change. I can see now that God's call on my life has always been music ministry, but at that time I really wanted to do both music and baseball. Baseball and music ministry, however, were about to have a head-on collision.

Our baseball team had a makeup game one day that simply had to be played on Sunday morning. That was very unusual, but Jacksonville State was in town and there was simply no other time for the game to be played.

I was committed to lead worship that morning at the church I attended. I had pitched the day before, so I knew my role with the baseball team on that particular day was to sit in the bull pen and cheer for our team. Since there really was no chance that I would play on Sunday, I figured I was good to go—break out the hymnals and warm up the choir!

Unfortunately my coach didn't see things the same way. He wanted me to be at the game. I felt that *both* baseball and music ministry were crucial to me, but the fact was that something had to take a back-seat. I didn't realize it at the time, but God was working through my circumstances; and I was about to make a major adjustment in my life.

As I prayed about the situation, I just couldn't find any peace about leaving 125 folks without a worship leader on Sunday morning. Trust me, I tried to find a way around the predicament, but it finally came down to a decision: something had to be sacrificed, and the time was now.

As I led worship that morning, I was so encouraged to see two familiar but unexpected faces in the congregation sitting close to my mom and dad. The parents of the pitcher for Jacksonville State—the starting pitcher in the game being played that morning—had heard about my decision, and they chose to join me in worship while their own son played the game! I honestly don't remember who won the game that day, but I clearly see now that God won the battle for my heart and my life.

In the days ahead the response to my decision was difficult to handle. Across the campus people were talking about what I had done and ridiculing my choice. I felt alone and distant from my coach and team. God used special people in my life, including my future wife, Teresa, to encourage me through that week. After a week or so, I was reinstated to the team and moved on. But something had happened in my life that changed me forever.

Years later I happened to be listening to the radio as I drove through Mississippi. My old coach at Delta State was being interviewed as he was being inducted into the Mississippi Sports Hall of Fame. I had always assumed that I let him down that day, and that thought left me with such an empty feeling. But there he was on the radio years later talking about his former players, including me! He told the audience that I was a minister and one of the finest young men he had ever coached. God reached out through that radio and gave me closure that day. Through my tears of appreciation, I realized that what had been a sacrifice in my mind on that special Sunday morning turned out to be the launching pad that God had planned for the rest of my life.

We all have found ourselves at similar crossroads in life—possibly laying down something that we want to have or to do in order to follow the "still small voice" of the Spirit. But more often, complete surrender means surrendering our hearts, our thoughts, and our reactions to the daily issues of life to God's direction. It isn't always easy to exchange our lives for His, but the rewards are indeed great when we do. As Jesus said,

> *"For whoever wants to save his life will lose it, but whoever loses his life because of Me will find it." (Matt. 16:25)*

Jesus has already made the supreme sacrifice of real flesh and blood on our behalf. Yet we must *choose* to surrender or yield our own bodies as instruments of righteousness, rather than instruments of our own selfish desires.

A Renewed Mind—The First Step

You *can* present your body as a living sacrifice, but that process starts with a reborn spirit and a mind that is continually being transformed or renewed by the Word of God:

> *Do not be conformed to this age, but be transformed by the renewing of your mind, so that you may discern what is the good, pleasing, and perfect will of God. (Rom. 12:2)*
>
> *Therefore, ridding yourselves of all moral filth and evil excess, humbly receive the implanted word, which is able to save you. (James 1:21)*

As born-again believers, we have the Spirit of Christ dwelling in us to guide and direct us, but we must train our minds and our bodies to respond to His direction in every situation. This training process begins with the renewing of our minds—reprogramming our thought life—which can happen only as we meditate on God's Word. This process takes time—a lifetime, in fact—but the result is a life that is good and acceptable to God. Even as you wake every morning, focus on the things that are "praiseworthy."

Finally brothers, whatever is true, whatever is honorable, whatever is just, whatever is pure, whatever is lovely, whatever is commendable—if there is any moral excellence and if there is any praise—dwell on these things. (Phil. 4:8)

Call to Worship

The Word of God is the only thing that can renew our minds, and it will contradict our minds regularly. The key is found in preferring God's Word to our own thoughts, and this a conscious decision on our part—often minute-by-minute. But God's thoughts really are higher and better than ours!

"For My thoughts are not your thoughts, and your ways are not My ways."
This is the LORD's declaration.
"For as heaven is higher than earth, so My ways are higher than your ways, and My thoughts than your thoughts."
(Isa. 55:8–9)

It takes revelation and a renewed mind to appreciate fully all that God is and has done in our lives. As we make a conscious decision to train our minds to align with His thoughts and His words of life, we are ready to adopt a lifestyle of worship.

Reflections

- Our response to God's love should be to express love to God and to others, which requires putting our love into action through service.
- Acts of loving service are not enough apart from complete surrender. In light of who God is and what He has done, our only reasonable response is to fully surrender our hearts and our lives to God.

- We can become a living sacrifice to God by laying down our desires and taking up God's desires moment by moment.

Prayer

*Dear Lord, thank You for the privilege of serving You.
Forgive me when my worship becomes a chore and my service
becomes a duty. Help me experience the power of serving
You with a worshipper's heart! Amen.*

22

A Lifestyle of Worship

*A lifestyle of worship is essential if we are
to overcome in order to "become."*

Laying down our lives in response to God's love cannot be relegated to a weekly worship service. Yes, it is important to gather God's people in worship. That is our time to enter His presence corporately, hear the Word, and be energized to go back into the world and live for Christ. Our corporate worship is essential, but it is not enough.

Worship must be part of our everyday lives if we are to become living sacrifices—not conformed to the world, but transformed by the renewing of our minds (see Rom. 12:2). This renewal takes time, attention, and energy. It is a daily process, and one that is not easy. In fact, it often is a struggle— a struggle against virtually every force we encounter in our daily lives.

Recognizing and Preparing for the Battle

There is an enemy of God, and therefore an enemy of ours, who wants to steal, kill, and destroy our lives. The apostle Paul explains the battle this way:

*For our battle is not against flesh and blood, but against
the rulers, against the authorities, against the world powers of this darkness, against the spiritual forces of evil in the
heavens. (Eph. 6:12)*

The battleground is clear: our bodies will become a living sacrifice on one altar or the other—either to God or to the world system.
God so loved the world that He gave all we need to overcome, but we
must respond. This involves two things: First, we must recognize and
acknowledge the battle for the conformity of our minds and our lives.
Second, we must be equipped to overcome those powers and principalities that assault us and our families, fellow believers around the world,
and our nation.

We have been given exactly what we need for the battle—God's
armor. With His armor in place, we really can stand against the adversary. Paul describes the armor of God in his letter to the Ephesians:

*This is why you must take up the full armor of God, so that
you may be able to resist in the evil day, and having prepared
everything, to take your stand. Stand, therefore, with truth
like a belt around your waist, righteousness like armor on your
chest, and your feet sandaled with readiness for the gospel
of peace. In every situation take the shield of faith, and with
it you will be able to extinguish the flaming arrows of the evil
one. Take the helmet of salvation, and the sword of the Spirit,
which is God's word. (Eph. 6:13–17)*

There are many wonderful books and Bible studies available that
can help us learn more about the armor of God, but for now let us consider another powerful tool that can help us to stand against the enemy
of our faith—worship! Our expression of worship always invites God's
intervention in our circumstances.

Worshipping in the Midst of the Battle

As we worship, our attention is focused clearly on God, recognizing that He is our provider and our defender. Our response of worship
in even the most difficult situations invites the presence of the Lord;
and when God is present, we cannot fail.

The story of King Jehoshaphat in 2 Chronicles 20 provides a great
picture of worship as an intentional response in the midst of warfare.

God's people were in serious trouble. They were facing a great multitude who wanted to exterminate them from the earth. Now that is warfare!

Read More about It

- Judah is threatened: 2 Chronicles 20:1–2
- The people fast and seek God's help: 2 Chronicles 20:3–4
- Jehoshaphat prays and worships in the assembly: 2 Chronicles 20:5–12
- Jahaziel receives a word from the Lord: 2 Chronicles 20:13–17
- The people worship: 2 Chronicles 20:18–21
- God responds: 2 Chronicles 20:22–23
- Judah is victorious and rejoices: 2 Chronicles 20:24–30

Jehoshaphat declared a fast throughout all of Judah and gathered the people together to pray and ask help from the Lord. As they assembled in the house of the Lord, Jehoshaphat began to worship God, proclaiming His greatness and recalling all that God had done for them. Notice that their first response to the threats of the enemy was prayer and worship!

As the king worshipped, he declared, "Nor do we know what to do, *but* our eyes are upon You" (2 Chron. 20:12 NKJV, emphasis added). As they focused on the One whom they served and worshipped, God inhabited their worship and spoke through one of the worship leaders. God's strategy was clear: He was sending them out simply to stand in the presence of their enemies and watch God work. The worshippers went first into the battlefield, and they led Israel to complete victory!

Jehoshaphat and all of Judah responded to God's revelation spoken prophetically that day with worship:

> Then Jehoshaphat bowed with his face to the ground [shachach], and all Judah and the inhabitants of Jerusalem fell down before the LORD to worship Him. Then the Levites . . . stood up to praise the LORD God of Israel shouting in a loud voice. (2 Chron. 20:18–19)

True to God's direction, Jehoshaphat sent the worshippers ahead of the army. As God's children began to sing and worship, the Lord miraculously defeated their enemies:

> The moment they began their shouts and praises, the LORD set an ambush against the Ammonites, Moabites, and the inhabitants of Mount Seir who came to fight against Judah, and they were defeated. (2 Chron. 20:22)

What had looked like a battle with flesh and blood was won in the spirit world *and* in the natural world as they responded to God's revelation with worship!

Jehoshaphat's story here can be a clear and consistent guide to our worship life. Let's summarize the key points:

1. The odds were certainly against God's people. Jehoshaphat was facing a *multitude* who had determined to wipe God's people off the face of the earth. (v. 2)
2. Jehoshaphat responded with prayer and worship. He proclaimed a *fast* throughout all Judah. (v. 3)
3. He gathered the people together to *seek* the Lord. (v. 4)
4. He stood in the *assembly* and lifted his voice to God. (v. 5)
5. Circumstances were overwhelming, but God was worshipped and exalted in the assembly. Jehoshaphat concluded, "But our eyes are upon *You*." (v. 12)
6. True to His promise, God inhabited the praises of His people that day. He revealed who He was and what He was going to do in the situation. He told them that they would not need to *fight* in this battle but that He would deliver them. (v. 17)
7. The people responded with more *worship*. (v. 18)

If you are facing an "impossible" circumstance in your life, follow Jehoshaphat's lead: pray, fast, worship, receive the word of the Lord, and take action.

Call to Worship

We have much to learn from this story. We, like the Israelites, worship the One who made us for worship, the One who redeemed us from our sinful nature and from death itself. We worship in response to God's revelation. We make an informed decision to surrender to His love and become a living sacrifice, holy and pleasing to Him. That is our reasonable service. As we worship in the midst of the battle, God has promised His presence; and He will give us the grace and the strategy to overcome the adversary in our lives!

Reflections

- Laying down our lives for God and becoming a living sacrifice must be a daily process.
- Our lives will become a living sacrifice either to God or to the world system.
- There is an enemy of God who wants to steal, kill, and destroy our lives.
- We must recognize and acknowledge the battle for the conformity of our minds and our lives, and we must be equipped to overcome those powers and principalities that assault us.
- We have been given exactly what we need for the battle: God's armor.
- Our response to the threats of the adversary starts with prayer and worship.
- God reveals His strategy for our lives as we pray, and He implements that strategy as we worship Him—for who He is and what He has done!
- Our response of worship in even the most difficult situations invites the presence of the Lord; and when God is present, we cannot fail.

Prayer

Dear Lord, I sing this song to You:
As I live today would you give me grace
To embrace my cross and die to me?
When the arrows fly, I won't question why
And just embrace my cross and die to me
I want to know you in your suffering
So resurrection power can rule my life
Lord I humbly pray help me choose today
To embrace my cross and die to me.
Amen.

23

Worship and the Word

Worship strengthens the Word in us.

As we respond to the revelation of God's great love by laying down our lives—as we become a living sacrifice—we can always expect resistance. Worship is our response to the revelation of God, and there is a heavenly battle that always centers around worship. That is one reason why worship is such a divisive element in many churches today.

As we saw in the story of King Jehoshaphat, we are equipped for battle through prayer, fasting, worship, and the Word of God. The battle is won in prayer; our strength and encouragement are found in the presence of the Lord as we worship; and the Word of God is our mighty weapon—the sword of the Spirit—with which we take the offensive:

> *Take the helmet of salvation, and the sword of the Spirit, which is God's word. With every prayer and request, pray at all times in the Spirit, and stay alert in this, with all perseverance and intercession for all the saints. (Eph. 6:17–18)*

A Powerful Combination

God's Word and worship are indeed a powerful combination.

For the word of God is living and effective and sharper
than any two-edged sword, penetrating as far as to divide
soul, spirit, joints, and marrow; it is a judge of the ideas and
thoughts of the heart. No creature is hidden from Him, but all
things are naked and exposed to the eyes of Him to whom we
must give an account. (Heb. 4:12–13)

In worship we both receive the Word of God and strengthen the Word within us. Worship apart from the revelation of the Word (the Living Word and written Word) is incomplete. But worship in response to God's revelation brings that Word to life in a powerful way. Worship and the Word go hand-in-hand, and this powerful combination is a crucial element in living the abundant life that Jesus promised:

"I have come that they may have life and have it in
abundance." (John 10:10)

The world we live in is full of struggles, fears, and temptations. Jesus, the Living Word—the Living Two-Edged Sword—faced them all in the wilderness. He was tempted just as we are in every way, yet He was without sin. His response to the adversary is our example to follow:

Again, the Devil took to a very high mountain and showed
Him all the kingdoms of the world and their splendor. And
he said to Him, "I will give You all these things if You will fall
down and worship me." Then Jesus told him, "Go away,
Satan! For it is written: 'Worship the Lord your God, and serve
only Him.'" Then the Devil left Him, and immediately angels
came and began to serve Him. (Matt. 4:8–11)

The battleground was temptation, but the core issue was worship. The enemy wanted Jesus to worship something other than God, but Jesus drew upon the Word of God within to fight the battle.

Nothing has changed since the time when Jesus was in the wilderness. The enemy still wants us to worship something other than God—Father, Son, and Spirit—and the answer to this and every other challenge or temptation is still, *It is written!* The Word of God is always the answer.

As we have seen previously, faith comes by hearing and hearing by the Word of God. Prayer prepares us for the battle, and worship strengthens the Word that has been deposited in us—often giving us new revelation or understanding of the Word.

Revelation in the Midst of Worship

Have you ever found yourself singing a worship chorus or a great hymn—possibly one you have sung many, many times—and suddenly you recognize another truth of God that had eluded you previously? That is the picture of revelation in the midst of worship.

The song "Praise the Lord," written by Brown Bannister and Mike Hudson and popularized by the Imperials, is a great example of revelation coming in the midst of worship. You see, every time I sing this song, I'm reminded of so many biblical truths. Just take a look at the insights this one verse brings (note the italicized lyrics):

Now *Satan is a liar*
And he wants to make us think
That we are paupers
When he knows himself
We're children of the King.
So lift up the mighty shield of faith
For the battle has been won.
We know that *Jesus Christ has risen*
So the work's already done.
Praise the Lord,
He can work through those who praise Him,
Praise the Lord
For *our God inhabits praise,*
Praise the Lord
For the chains that seem to bind you
Serve only to remind you that they drop powerless
    behind you
When you praise Him.[1]

Call to Worship

This is the reason we gather as the body of Christ—to receive more and more revelation. And this is why we also must "gather within ourselves" daily to receive the Word. Worship is the key. Every time we worship, we strengthen the Word that is in us and open ourselves to receive further revelation as well. And the Word of God never, ever fails, as this verse written by the prophet Isaiah tells us:

> *"For just as rain and snow fall from heaven, and do not return there without saturating the earth, and making it germinate and sprout, and providing seed to sow and food to eat, so My word that comes from My mouth will not return to Me empty, but it will accomplish what I please, and will prosper in what I send it to do." (Isa. 55:10–11)*

I encourage you to pause right now and sing your favorite worship chorus or hymn. As you sing, focus on the reinforcement that the words provide for the Word within you. *Worship indeed strengthens the Word in us!*

Reflections

- We are equipped for spiritual battle through prayer, fasting, worship, and the Word.
- Worship and the Word of God are a powerful combination!
- Worship strengthens the Word that has been deposited in us, often giving us new revelation or understanding of the Word.
- The enemy wants us to worship something other than Jesus.
- The Word of God is always the answer to every test and trial.

Prayer

*Heavenly Father, You have exalted above all things
Your name and Your Word. I cannot love one without
loving the other. Give me a deep desire to know Your Word
and honor Your name. Amen.*

Notes

1. "Praise the Lord" by Brown Banister and Mike Hudson, 1978 Word Music, LLC.

24

Worshipping While
We Wait

*Worshipping God while we are waiting for Him to act
opens a place for Him to intervene.*

We were made for relationship with God. He came down to us, met us at our point of need for a Savior, and He has chosen to dwell in and among us through His Holy Spirit. Our worship makes a place for His enthronement in our midst.

God wants us to respond to His love by worshipping Him even in the midst of the battles, struggles, and problems we face in life, making a place for Him to intervene. Sometimes His intervention is immediate, as it was for King Jehoshaphat and the Israelites, and sometimes we have to allow "patience [to] have its perfect work" as we wait expectantly for God to step into our difficult circumstances:

> Consider it a great joy, my brothers, whenever you experience
> various trials, knowing that the testing of your faith produces
> endurance. But endurance must do its complete work, so that
> you may be mature and complete, lacking nothing.
> (James 1:2–4)

You may be facing some very serious issues in your life right now. And frankly, it's difficult to feel like worshipping God at times. From time to time we all must make a decision: What will we do while we wait on the Lord?

My wife, Teresa, and I learned a great deal about God's grace through her battle with cancer—and we learned about worshipping in the midst of our hardships, as well.

I remember the day we got the cancer diagnosis like it was yesterday. The results of the biopsy weren't good. Jim Futral, pastor of the church we were serving in Jackson, Mississippi, was with us. I looked at Jim with tears in my eyes. Teresa had breast cancer, and it was the aggressive kind.

I left Jim for a few moments and walked out into the hall, not knowing what to do next. I would be the one to tell Teresa when she woke up, and likely the one to tell the kids. It was a very difficult moment, to say the least.

As I walked through the hall, I began to hear in my head the lyrics of a song I had written with a dear friend just a few weeks earlier:

Bow the knee. Trust the heart of your Father.
When the answer goes beyond what you can see,
Bow the knee.
Bow the knee. Lift your eyes toward heaven.
And believe the One who holds eternity.
When you don't understand the purpose of His plan,
In the presence of your King, bow the knee![1]

I didn't realize it at the time, but I had begun to worship God in the midst of our difficulties—to worship while we were "under the weight" of the problem.

When Teresa woke up and saw my face, she immediately knew the results of the biopsy. Sadly my brokenness revealed my lack of faith at that moment. I was a mess, but Teresa spoke very clearly: "So God must know that our faith is strong enough to handle a trial like this." Teresa had a revelation of who God is and what He had done in her life, and she wasn't about to let go!

As the days went by, we had to make many decisions about medical options and the surgeries that would come. But the best decision we made, right in the midst of the most difficult problem we ever tried to navigate, was to trust God. We decided to worship while we waited and while we were "under the weight" of the problem. We didn't always feel like worshipping, for sure, but with the loving support of the body of Christ, we walked the journey before us and received mercy at the throne of God's grace:

> *For we do not have a high priest who is unable to sympathize with our weaknesses, but One who has been tested in every way as we are, yet without sin. Therefore let us approach the throne of grace with boldness, so that we may receive mercy and find grace to help us at the proper time. (Heb. 4:15–16)*

Through the process, we learned a lot about ourselves, our God, our deep need to worship Him, and the depth of His love for us. As He revealed Himself further in response to our need, our worship continued to grow.

We found out that God is indeed a good God who loves us with an everlasting love. As we worshipped, we were reaching out to our loving heavenly Father who can change hearts, minds, and circumstances. The process began with Him, but we were required to respond. We learned firsthand that worship should always be our response to God's revelation.

Teresa was right—our faith had grown to the point where we could handle this extreme test. With the loving support of our family and church family, we walked through the surgeries with confidence and faith in our truly great God—regardless of the outcome. As we worshipped, He once again proved Himself worthy of our praise. And eleven years later, we are still worshipping God for who He is and what He has done!

As we honor God's Word, presenting our bodies as a living sacrifice, God does, indeed, respond to our expression of worship. The cycle is set in motion:

We are all part of the fallen human race in need of redemption.

God responded to our need and showed His love for us in Christ Jesus.

We respond to God's love through sacrificial living and worship.

God responds to our worship with His presence.
And when the King is present, all things are possible!

Call to Worship

Now, dear saint of the living God, set aside all else and lift your voice in worship! Pray the prayer below, invite the King of kings to intervene in your situation(s). He will never forsake you. Worship Him now—and throughout the time you are "under the weight" of these issues. He has promised to be present with you as you worship. Remember, when the King is present, all things are possible!

Reflections

- We can worship while we wait on God's answer or intervention in every situation we face, even while we are "under the weight" of our difficulties.
- Our appropriate response to who God is and what He has done for us is *always* worship.
- We honor God by presenting ourselves as a living sacrifice— devoted to sacrificial living and worship.

Prayer

Lord, You already know about my needs. And I'm coming to the throne of grace once again to receive mercy.
I need You! Lord Jesus, as I lift my specific needs to You, I'm asking You for answers and solutions to each one.
I acknowledge You as Lord over my life, and I trust You— and You alone—as my Savior. I will worship You while I wait for Your intervention. Lord, give me the faith to trust You even when I don't understand You. You don't put me through circumstances—You bring me through them. Let me worship You in every circumstance for Your glory. Amen.

Notes

1. "Bow the Knee" written by Christopher Machen and Mike Harland, ©1999 Centergetic Music (ASCAP). All Rights Reserved. Used by Permission. International Copyright Secured.

25

Freedom in Worship

God wants us to worship Him with all our heart and soul.

We all face tests and trials on a regular basis. Tests and trials are just a part of the process of life. The issue is not the type or magnitude of any one trial we face, but our response to every test. God's Word gives us real hope *and* real direction as we respond. Let's take another look at this passage from the book of James:

> Consider it a great joy, my brothers, whenever you experience various trials, knowing that the testing of your faith produces endurance. But endurance must do its complete work, so that you may be mature and complete, lacking nothing.
> Now if any of you lacks wisdom, he should ask God, who gives to all generously and without criticizing, and it will be given to him. (James 1:2–5)

God is a rewarder of those who diligently seek Him, as Hebrews 11:6 tells us. He is the author of our salvation and our hope. Every moment we spend in His presence and in the written Word strengthens the hope that has been deposited in us as believers. And as hope increases—as we are filled with a hope that will never disappoint—we can function as the body of Christ was designed to function: glorifying God with our response of worship.

> For whatever was written before was written for our instruction, so that through our endurance and through the encouragement of the Scriptures we may have hope. Now may the God of endurance and encouragement grant you agreement with one another, according to Christ Jesus, so that you may glorify the God and Father of our Lord Jesus Christ with a united mind and voice. (Rom. 15:4–6)

Worshipping Fully and Freely

Have you ever wondered what it would be like to have no limitations as you respond to God? I have. My desire for unhindered worship in my own life continues to grow as I understand more and more about who God is and what He has already done in my life. Experiencing the intervention of God in the cancer trial that Teresa and I shared brought us to a greater freedom in worship. When God met us at the throne of grace and intervened on our behalf, our only reasonable and adequate response was—and is and always will be—worship!

Whether we are worshipping corporately or privately, our response to God should be biblically based and unhindered. Yet within these two general parameters, we all have socially and culturally familiar elements in our worship. Our childhood training and the worship we have experienced throughout our lives often dictate how freely we respond to God.

Some members of the body cry out loudly or prostrate themselves on the floor. Some wave flags and banners of adulation and praise, while others sing hymns or worship choruses or gather quietly in solemn assembly. The style of worship, the volume of worship, and the elements of worship are not the issue. The issue is that each believer must raise his or her own unhindered expression of worship to the King of kings in response to what He alone has done.

God made each member of His body, and He wants to hear our heartfelt expressions of praise. He wants us to worship with all our heart and soul—without reservation! When I think of that kind of worship, I think of Miss Bessie.

Worshipping without Reservation

I visit my home church, Oakland Baptist Church in Corinth, Mississippi, from time to time, but I will never forget one of my visits at Christmastime just a few years ago. I grew up at Tate Street Baptist Church but joined Oakland when I was in college, and it seems that Bessie Nelms—Miss Bessie to most of us kids—was always at the church. Miss Bessie was what I would call the matriarch of the church. She constantly served the body of Christ there in Corinth, and everybody knew her.

On the way to church that Christmas, my mother told me that Miss Bessie had been diagnosed with throat cancer. She had openly shared her dilemma at a recent testimonial service at the church, so it was no secret.

At that testimonial service Miss Bessie had told the congregation that she would likely lose her voice, and that was a *big* deal! You see, I had led worship at Oakland many times. And Miss Bessie was always near the front, singing and praising God with a loud voice. She wasn't the best singer in the world, but I promise you, Miss Bessie was a worshipper!

When she shared the likelihood that she would lose her voice, she wanted the congregation—her friends for life—to know that she just couldn't stop worshipping God, even though she would no longer be able to sing. Miss Bessie wanted to be sure it was OK with her friends if she raised her hands in worship when she could no longer lift her voice of praise.

A year later I visited the church, and sure enough Miss Bessie had lost her voice completely. But true to her word, she was right there on the front row, raising her hands and glorifying her King of kings.

Miss Bessie simply had to worship! It was in her, and it had to come out of her. She had had a lifetime of revelation and experience with her God and Savior. She had chosen to surrender her life fully to the Lord, and worship—along with service—was indeed her "rational and reasonable response" to her God.

Only a few short weeks later, Miss Bessie changed residences—she moved her place of worship from the front row of the church to the front row of heaven. Oakland had always been a worshipping congregation, but we all learned to experience greater freedom in worship from our dear hero of the faith. She taught us what it means to worship God without reservation.

The Bible is full of specific activities of worship, including those listed below. Some of these you have *witnessed* during worship services you have attended. Some you may have *experienced* personally. And some you may be secretly *longing to experience* as you respond to God's revelation. Meditate on this list, refer to the Scriptures, and pray for your freedom to worship.

- Kneeling/bowing (2 Chron. 29:29; Luke 22:41; Acts 20:36)
- Singing (Pss. 100:2; 147:1, 7; Eph. 5:19; Col. 3:16)
- Praying (Matt. 6:9–13; Acts 1:14; 4:31; 1 Thess. 5:17)
- Shouting (Pss. 95:1–2; 98:8; Zech. 9:9)
- Clapping (Pss. 47:1; 98:8; Isa. 55:12)
- Prostrating (Deut. 9:18; Josh. 5:14; 1 Kings 18:39; Rev. 1:17)
- Raising hands (2 Chron. 6:13; Ps. 63:4; 1 Tim. 2:8)
- Dancing (2 Sam. 6:14; Pss. 30:11; 149:3)
- Playing instruments (1 Chron. 15:16; Pss. 98:5–6; 150:3–5)
- Meditating/listening (Josh. 1:8; Ps. 77:12; 81:13; 119:15; Prov. 19:20; Phil. 4:8)
- Giving (Isa. 58:7; Mal. 3:10; 2 Cor. 9:7)
- Serving (Ps. 100:2; Matt. 20:25–28; Acts 20:19; Rom. 12:1; 1 Cor. 9:19)
- Taking communion (Mark 14:22–26; Luke 22:19–20; 1 Cor. 11:23–26)
- Fasting (Neh. 1:4; Esther 4:3; Isa. 58; Daniel 9:3; Joel 2:12)

> *Now the Lord is the Spirit; and where the Spirit of the Lord is, there is freedom. (2 Cor. 3:17)*

Call to Worship

Miss Bessie would have fit in quite well during Jesus' triumphal entry into Jerusalem as He proceeded toward His destiny at Calvary. It's not hard to imagine her standing by the road as Jesus entered the city—standing and waving her hands, uttering whatever sound she could make to proclaim the greatness of her King Jesus.

> *Now He came near the path down the Mount of Olives,*
> *and the whole crowd of the disciples began to praise God*
> *joyfully with a loud voice for all the miracles they had seen:*

*"'Blessed is the King who comes in the name of the
LORD!'
Peace in heaven and glory in the highest heaven!"
(Luke 19:37–38)*

That same Jesus is present with us right now. He went to the cross at Calvary and has overcome sin and death once and for all—for all of us. Our response must be unhindered worship!

Reflections

- Whether we are worshipping corporately or privately, our response to God should be biblically based and unhindered.
- We all have socially and culturally familiar elements in our worship; our childhood training and the worship we have experienced throughout our lives often dictate how freely we respond to God.
- The style of worship is not the issue. The issue is worshipping God fully and freely—with all one's heart and soul.
- Each believer must offer his or her own expression of unhindered worship to the King of kings.
- The "externals" of worship are just that—external. God looks on the heart.
- God wants to hear our heartfelt expressions of praise!

Prayer

Dear Father, forgive me when I "assess" the worship of others by what I see in worship. Help me remember that You look on my heart and the hearts of those around me. Amen.

EXPRESSION

Song of Worship

"Stand and Shout"

Stand and shout, shout and sing
We've been bought and redeemed
Jesus died, Jesus lives
Jesus loves and He forgives
So let your praise rise up and magnify
Let your voice be heard and testify

(Chorus)
Our God loves, our God saves
Our God rescues from the grave
Our God showers down His mercy
For the glory of His name
Our God heals, our God frees
Our God gives us everything
To live and love in freedom here and now
Stand and shout!

(Bridge)
I'm gonna stand and praise my God
My God has done mighty things for me
I'm gonna stand and praise my God
Stand and shout!

WORDS AND MUSIC BY TRAVIS COTTRELL & MIKE HARLAND
© 2007 VAN NESS PRESS, INC. (ASCAP) (ADMIN. BY LIFEWAY WORSHIP MUSIC
GROUP)/FIRST HAND REVELATION MUSIC (ADMIN. BY INTEGRITY MUSIC)

26

A Unique Expression

Each of us was **created** by God for relationship with Him, but we can only enjoy that relationship by God's **grace**. God's great **love** for us, demonstrated in Christ Jesus, initiates our **response**. The only reasonable and adequate response is our **expression** of worship.

God delights in our unique expressions of worship in response to His revelation.

We have seen that once we understand what God has done for us in Christ Jesus, worship really is our only rational and reasonable response. The God who made us loved us enough to sacrifice His own Son to fulfill the just penalty of the law. We are able to enter God's presence only by His grace—His unmerited favor and transforming power provided for our benefit. It is vitally clear that God is the One who is worthy of our worship.

"For God loved the world in this way: He gave His One and Only Son, so that everyone who believes in Him will not perish but have eternal life." (John 3:16)

Therefore, brothers, by the mercies of God, I urge you to present your bodies as a living sacrifice, holy and pleasing to God; this is your spiritual worship. (Rom. 12:1)

The Hebrew word for worship, *shachah*, provides a picture of someone bowing, kneeling, stooping, or prostrating on the ground in worship before God. The English word *worship* means to revere or adore God. In either case, worship comes from the one who is lesser and dependent as he or she understands and submits to the greatness of the One who is superior.

As we have emphasized throughout this book, worship is our response to God's revelation. Once we understand our human position relative to God's omnipotence and greatness, we are ready to become true worshippers. That understanding is what led Abraham to *shachah*, and that understanding can do the same for us.

Relationship Is the Key

Have you ever noticed that our own reaction to other people is based on our relative position to them—our relationship with them? For instance, when we encounter someone we don't know, we might nod or just smile as we pass by. If we see someone we know, we might extend a handshake or call the person's name. And if we have a meaningful relationship with someone, whether past or present, we might reach out and give the person a hug. However, if a person has been used in a special way by God to touch us intimately in a time of need or a great breakthrough, we just might throw our arms in the air and embrace our friend tightly as we express how much it means to see him or her.

As we worship, God has promised to be present; and like the encounters I've just described, we are likely to respond to His presence based on our past and present relationship with Him. Our willingness to spend time in His presence and invite Him into every aspect of our lives—surrendering ourselves as a living sacrifice—dictates how we respond as we encounter God.

Our worship expression is a clear indicator of the depth and quality of our relationship with God. When we live a surrendered life in response to who He is and what He has done, our response as we encounter God is *free and unhindered*. What someone else might think about our response really doesn't matter. Worship is truly all about Him!

Many Expressions of Worship

The way we express unhindered worship may take many forms. Whether we sing songs of praise from a hymnbook, raise a shout of acclamation, wave a flag, lift our hands, bow on our knees, play a drum, sing in a choir, or simply utter His name, God wants to see and hear our unique expressions of worship. He is interested in worship that comes from people who are being transformed by the truth of His Word and whose hearts are devoted to the one and only God.

The issue is not the style of worship; the issue is that each believer must raise his or her own expression of worship to the King of kings in response to what He alone has done. God wants to hear our unique expressions of praise. We simply cannot allow worship leaders to worship for us. They are expressing their worship, but God wants to hear our very own expressions of worship.

Unfortunately we often observe the worship expressions of others and measure their response to God's revelation by our own socially and culturally acceptable expressions of worship without really understanding why they respond to God the way they do. God, however, evaluates the heart of the worshipper, and that is important for us to remember.

> But the LORD said to Samuel, "Do not look at his appearance or his stature, because I have rejected him. Man does not see what the LORD sees, for man sees what is visible, but the LORD sees the heart." (1 Sam. 16:7)

The Bible: Our Worship Standard

We are all creatures of habit. Our tendency is to measure each new experience by a standard that has been established by our comfort level with previous experiences. Even the prophet Samuel struggled with this issue. Although his experience and logic told him to look for certain key attributes when selecting the next king of Israel, God's Spirit led him to look deeper. And ultimately he found the one God had selected to lead His people: David.

> ## Read More about It
>
> • Samuel anoints David as king: 1 Samuel 16:1–13

Standards are good as long as they are God's standards, and the Bible is filled with standards to guide our expression of worship. However, our tendency as human beings is to limit ourselves and those around us based on our own emotional comfort level. As a result, worship has in many ways been relegated to a tradition, an art form, and an experience. In reality, worship is an expression—the unhindered expression of our response to God's revelation!

It is crucial that we look to the Bible as our "standard" when it comes to expressing our worship. God's desire for us never contradicts His written Word, and His Word must be our guideline as we worship. The Bible provides both freedom and boundaries for authentic worship expression.

Call to Worship

In my role as worship leader for many congregations, I have seen countless believers express their heartfelt praise and adoration for the Lord. My own worship has been enhanced by precious saints who present their talents and abilities as a living sacrifice in the midst of worship. Whether that expression is singing, playing an instrument, sculpting, painting, dancing, or signing for the deaf, God delights in every sincere expression of worship. Every heartfelt expression of worship offered unto the Lord is precious in His sight. And God wants to hear and see *your unique expression* of praise and adoration:

> Let the word of Christ dwell in you richly in all wisdom, teaching and admonishing one another in psalms and hymns and spiritual songs, singing with grace in your hearts to the Lord. **And whatever you do in word or deed, do all in the name of the Lord Jesus, giving thanks to God the Father through Him.** (Col. 3:16–17 NKJV, emphasis added)

God desires that we worship Him in response to His revelation of who He is and what He has done! As the revelation of God grows in our hearts, God provides the grace to overcome our insecurities and concerns about what others think as we offer our unique expressions of worship to Him. God truly delights in the praises of His people, and He wants each of us to have complete freedom in worship.

Reflections

- Our worship expression is a clear indicator of the depth and quality of our relationship with God.
- When we live a surrendered life in response to who God is and what He has done, our response as we encounter God is free and unhindered.
- Our expression of worship can take many forms.
- The Bible provides many examples of worship expression.
- The only standard for worship that matters is God's standard—the guidelines found in His Word. The Bible must be our final authority as we worship.
- The Bible provides both freedom and boundaries for authentic worship expression.
- When we have true revelation of God in our hearts, we will overcome our insecurities and concerns about what others think as we worship Him.

Prayer

*Lord, remind me that You are my only audience in worship.
Help me express my worship, not for the sake of those
around me, but only for You. Amen.*

27

Expressing Worship through Music

*God created music and musicians to precede
and proclaim His presence, His power, and His Word;
and to prepare His people to receive Him.*

Worship is often expressed through a song. In fact, music and musicians were created for worship. In 1 and 2 Chronicles, we are given a clear picture of God's plan for musicians in corporate worship. Whether or not you are a musician, it is important for you as a worshipper to understand how God desires to use singers, musicians, and worship leaders in the local church.

Musicians in the House of the Lord

In the Old Testament, God set aside thirty-eight thousand Levites for His service in the temple. Their duties were numerous and ranged from ministering to the people and taking offerings to judging and making decisions when there were controversies (see 1 Chron. 23–26).

Read More about It

- David commanded the Levites to appoint their kindred as musicians: 1 Chronicles 15:16–24
- Musicians preceded the ark of the covenant: 1 Chronicles 15:25–28
- David stationed singers and musicians around the ark in the tabernacle: 1 Chronicles 16:4
- The singers, musicians, and people praised the Lord: 1 Chronicles 16:7–36
- Music is a part of regular worship: 1 Chronicles 16:37–43
- David appointed four thousand temple musicians: 1 Chronicles 23:5

Of those thirty-eight thousand Levites, four thousand (more than 10 percent) were appointed by King David as musicians. Music must be important to God!

Prior to the building of the temple, when the ark of the covenant—the resident place of God's power, presence, and Word— was brought from the house of Obed-edom to the tabernacle in Jerusalem, King David commanded the chiefs of the Levites to appoint their kindred as musicians. Since these musical Levites were selected by their peers, talent and skill certainly must have been a consideration. It was at that time that the musician's role was clearly defined:

> David, the elders of Israel, and the commanders of the thousands went with rejoicing to bring the ark of the covenant of the LORD from the house of Obed-edom. And because God helped the Levites who were carrying the ark of the covenant of the LORD, they sacrificed seven bulls and seven rams.
>
> Now David was dressed in a robe of fine linen, as were all the Levites who were carrying the ark, as well as the singers and Chenaniah, the music leader of the singers. David also wore a linen ephod. So all Israel was bringing the ark of the covenant of the LORD up with shouts, the sound of the ram's horn, trumpets, and cymbals, and the playing of harps and lyres. (1 Chron. 15:25–28)

As the musicians led the procession, the purpose for which they were created was revealed:

God created music and musicians to precede and proclaim His presence, His power, and His Word; and to prepare His people to receive Him.

Shortly thereafter, King David created the "first church music department" when he stationed the singers and musicians around the ark of the covenant:

David appointed some of the Levites to be ministers before the ark of the LORD, to celebrate the LORD God of Israel, and to give thanks and praise to Him. (1 Chron. 16:4)

In so doing, the rest of God's purpose for musicians was revealed:

God created music and musicians to lead His people as they celebrate, thank, and praise the Lord.

God did not create and appoint musicians to worship for the people, but to lead the people as they worshipped! God wasn't interested in a worship experience for the people to sit back and enjoy. He set the musicians in place to lead the people in their own expression of worship. But, this awesome responsibility was about a great deal more than music. First Chronicles 25:1 says: "David and the officers of the army also set apart some of the sons of Asaph, Heman, and Jeduthun, who were to prophesy accompanied by lyres, harps, and cymbals." I often tell worship leaders that this verse has the three-word job description for the church musician—*Preach with accompaniment.* I've heard some say that theology in worship isn't important and that we should just focus on the expression of praise. I could not disagree more. What more can we offer to the Lord than to declare His greatness in our worship? There is a place for expressing how we feel about God in our worship. But if that's all we do, I'm afraid our worship will have little impact on our lives.

Think of it this way: If I spent all my energy while I was dating Teresa telling her how I felt about her without ever saying what it is about her that makes me love her, I'm not sure my courtship would have accomplished much. But when I said, "I love you because you are beautiful and kind, talented, smart, and sweet, and because you have shown so much love for me." I could go on, but I think you get the idea. And, as I'm saying those things I know are true, I am learning even more about her and loving her more.

Read More about It

- Solomon dedicated the temple and the people worshipped: 2 Chronicles 5–7:3

Musicians Lead the People's Expression of Worship

The same process of worship was repeated at the dedication of the temple under King Solomon. However, this time, as the musicians fulfilled their purpose in preceding the power, presence, and Word of God, the presence of the Lord fell on the people in such might that the whole service was disrupted:

> The trumpeters and singers joined together to praise and thank the LORD with one voice. They raised their voices, accompanied by trumpets, cymbals, and musical instruments, in praise to the LORD:
> "For He is good:
> His faithful love endures forever;"
> the temple, the LORD's temple, was filled with a cloud. And because of the cloud, the priests were not able to continue ministering, for the glory of the LORD filled God's temple. (2 Chron. 5:13–14)

The singers and musicians were one—harmonically and spiritually—and the King of kings responded with His presence! Now that's what I want to see in our worship assemblies, don't you?

Call to Worship

Music is a great gift from God. Music and musicians serve a crucial purpose in our worship expression. In this era of recorded music and digital transmission through radio, television, cell phones, iPods, and computers, we have access to great worship music that can lead us into God's presence throughout each day. Those recordings are often the work of musicians who are fulfilling their purpose in leading each of us into worship, praise, and celebration.

I know from personal experience that playing worship music, even on days when I don't feel like worshipping, leads me into God's presence. As you have opportunity to listen to worship music, be sure and join the musicians and raise your voice of worship.

So sing along, and sing loud! Proclaim God's love, goodness, greatness, and imminent return. Don't allow the stones or even the finest musicians to worship for you! God created you for worship, and He loves to hear *your* unique expression of praise.

Reflections

- Music is important to God.
- God created music and musicians to precede and proclaim His power, presence, and Word—preparing the hearts of His people to receive Him.
- Musicians lead God's people as they celebrate, thank, and praise Him.
- God wants to hear every voice of praise and worship!

Prayer

Thank You, Lord, for creating music and giving it to us as a way to worship You. Lord, may music not be the focus of our worship, but just a way to express our growing praise of You. Amen.

28

The True Worship Leader

God created singers and musicians to be "lead worshippers,"
but the pastor is the true worship leader.

Singers and musicians play a crucial part in leading the people to express their hearts in worship and to receive the power, presence, and Word of God. We commonly refer to the leader of a group of worshippers as the worship leader. However, we must be careful not to overlook the *true worship leader.*

Consider these two examples from the Old Testament:

> David assembled all Israel at Jerusalem to bring the ark of the LORD to the place he had prepared for it. . . .
>
> Then David told the leaders of the Levites to appoint their relatives as singers and to have them raise their voices with joy accompanied by musical instruments—harps, lyres, and cymbals. (1 Chron. 15:3, 16)
>
> At that time Solomon assembled at Jerusalem the elders of Israel—all the tribal heads, the ancestral chiefs of the Israelites—in order to bring the ark of the covenant of the LORD up from the city of David, that is, Zion. . . .

Then Solomon stood before the altar of the LORD in front
of the entire congregation of Israel . . .
When Solomon finished praying, fire descended from
heaven and consumed the burnt offering and the sacrifices,
and the glory of the LORD filled the temple. (2 Chron. 5:2;
6:12; 7:1)

The model God gave us for worship includes a major role for the singers and musicians. But the true worship leader in each of these instances was the one who presided over the whole event. In the first example, the worship leader was King David; in the second, the worship leader was King Solomon. Presiding over such gatherings was part of the king's role as the spiritual leader of the nation of Israel. Similarly, the one who presides over the worship service today should be the spiritual leader of the congregation.

The Pastor as Worship Leader

We commonly refer to the music leader or minister of music as the worship leader, but the true worship leader is the spiritual leader of the church: the pastor. Every part of the worship service must be under the pastor's authority and direction. The pastor is the one who is charged by God with the overall welfare of God's precious lambs, *including* God's servant who is in charge of the music.

Singers and musicians have a very specific purpose in worship: to prepare our hearts to receive the Word. They are created and called to be "lead worshippers," and that is a crucial role in the worship life of the church. But again, it is the pastor who is the true leader in worship. When this distinction is clearly understood, the congregation benefits greatly.

I have served in full-time worship ministry in seven churches across the southern part of the United States; and now as Director of Worship for LifeWay Christian Resources, I regularly attend worship services and interact with pastors and music leadership across the country. One thing I have observed is that when the pastor and music minister or leader understand who is the true worship leader and work together, walking in unity, the songs selected for a worship service support and strengthen the Word of God that is preached or taught in the service.

In 1 Chronicles 16 David, God's appointed leader, was in charge of the whole worship service (which lasted for several days). The singers and musicians were crucial to the service. They were the lead worshippers. But the ark of the covenant—the resident place of the power, presence, and Word of God—was the centerpiece of worship. And the musicians were clearly directed by the true worship leader: King David.

I often explain the contemporary corporate worship experience this way: the pastor is to the worship service what the mother of the bride is to the wedding ceremony. If you've been to more than one wedding, you know what I mean. We all take our cues from the mother of the bride. When she stands, we stand. When she sits, we sit. When she leaves, we follow.

In the same way, members of the congregation take "worship cues" from the pastor. When the pastor is a worshipper and understands his role as worship leader, there is great freedom in worship.

Tom McCoy is such a pastor. Tom is the pastor of the church Teresa and I currently attend, Thompson Station Church. Tom and his wife, Leighann, have served the church for nearly twenty years. They started with a congregation of about twenty people; and when Teresa and I joined a few years ago, we became part of a church family of about two thousand people.

Tom truly understands his role as worship leader. Although we have a wonderful music program with great music leadership, I believe the key to this lies in the fact that Tom is a *worshipper*. I enjoy being in services with Tom because I know he is going to worship. Recently, during a powerful worship moment in our church, Tom walked up into the choir loft and stood by me in the middle of the choir. My eyes were closed, but suddenly I heard his voice and knew it was him. (I'll let you figure out how I knew it was him!). There I was singing with my pastor. And I sang all the more standing next to him. That is a perfect example of Tom's worship leading. It's not with his voice—it's with his worship! (I'll also let you figure out why I sang all the more!)

I've always been concerned whenever I see a pastor disengaged during the music, fumbling with his notes or talking to someone nearby. Without meaning to, such a pastor has a negative impact on the worship of his congregation. Make no mistake about it the senior pastor is the worship leader of his church. The worship expression of his people will rise and fall based on how he participates. I've seen it countless times.

That's why I'm so grateful that whether he is on the front row or on the platform, Tom's response to God's revelation is clear: he worships! And we all follow his lead. His response to God brings great freedom to all of us.

Call to Worship

I love attending worship services where the pastor and music leadership—the "lead worshippers"—are moving in unity. The impact on the congregation is obvious when leaders understand their God-given roles in the worship service. When they do, God's people truly are the beneficiaries.

If you are a pastor, I want to encourage you to worship with your congregation. I assure you, your outward expression of praise, adoration, and thanksgiving will create freedom in those under your care. They were made for worship, and so were you!

Reflections

- God created singers and musicians to be "lead worshippers."
- The pastor is the true worship leader.
- God's people will respond to the model of worship that the pastor demonstrates.
- God's people benefit as the pastor and lead worshippers are unified.

Prayer

God, thank You for those who lead worship in our churches. And thank You for my pastor, who leads our people in worship every week. Lord, help the pastors of our churches see the awesome responsibility they have to lead their people in worship. Amen.

29

Worshipping Together— The Corporate Worship Service

Four key parts of the worship service and one special element of worship can help us to express our worship.

As we have seen, music is a crucial part of the corporate worship service. Much more than a longstanding tradition, music fulfills a specific, God-ordained purpose in worship: it proclaims God's power, presence, and Word—preparing the hearts of His people to receive Him. Music is a vital element in many parts of the worship service, yet there is much more to the service.

Dr. Robert Webber, one of the most highly regarded teachers on worship of our day, broke the worship service into four major or distinct parts:

1. The Coming In
2. The Table of the Lord

3. The Proclamation of the Word

4. The Going Out

Let's briefly explore each of these parts of the worship service and how they help us to express our worship to God.

The Coming In

As we come into the sanctuary, we are literally and figuratively setting ourselves apart from the world. If you've ever tried to get a family of toddlers or teenagers to church on time, you understand how "worldly" Sunday mornings can be.

We have been out in the world; now we are coming into the house of God to encounter the King of kings. We sing at the beginning of the worship service because music and musicians were created to precede the power, presence, and Word of God. We sing as we separate ourselves from the world in order to prepare our hearts to encounter His presence.

In addition to singing, we also pray and read Scripture during this part of the worship service. The Coming In is our opportunity to fully turn our attention to the Lord—not something to get out of the way so that we can get on to the sermon! Once the coming in—the separating from the world—has occurred, we are ready to proceed with the worship service.

The Table of the Lord

The Table of the Lord is observed at different times during the worship service and with different frequency throughout the body of Christ. Whenever it occurs in the service, remembering the broken body and shed blood of Jesus Christ is indeed crucial to our worship. It is given as a visible reminder of God's eternal sacrifice in Christ Jesus.

The Lord's Table must never become a ritual or just a tradition. It is a vital and crucial worship expression. The shed blood and broken body of our Lord will never lose its power!

This was illustrated to me in a powerful way through two such observances separated by eighteen months. In the first one, my wife was sitting with our five-year-old son, John, during a Communion service. As the tray of unleavened bread approached, John reached out for a handful. Teresa quietly stopped him, to which he said loudly, "But

I'm hungry!" After the service we tried to explain why John was not allowed to participate.

Fast-forward eighteen months to the second service, which was the first such observance since John's profession of faith and baptism. I was next to him this time and as the bread approached, I noticed his attitude was solemn and reverent. He looked up at me and asked, "What do I do?" I helped my son retrieve his first piece of unleavened bread as a new believer. I explained to him that our pastor would lead us and show us when to partake. I added that as I wait, I like to pray and reflect on what Christ did for me. He seemed to understand. I'll admit this time I prayed with one eye open because I was watching him. He bowed his head and then I noticed a small tear rolling down his cheek as he prayed silently. Then a big tear rolled down mine! John's sensitivity to this observance that seemed so routine to me brought conviction to my heart. God used my son to help me see the richness of His table once again.

Whether we call it the Lord's Table, the Lord's Supper, or Communion, the Lord's Table continues to unite us. Whether we observe it weekly, monthly, or every now and then, remembering the broken body and shed blood of Jesus Christ is crucial to our worship. Jesus *is* the full revelation of God, and He initiates our response of worship. Jesus has been the center point of worship for the church throughout the centuries for good reason, and the table of the Lord brings our entire focus back to Him—inspiring further worship and proclamation of His gospel!

The Proclamation of the Word

The second part of the worship service is the proclamation of the Word of God. Have you ever noticed that a service of praise music without some proclamation of the Word just seems incomplete? That's because it *is* incomplete. Music was created to illustrate the Word, not to replace it. When we gather in God's name without the reading or the preaching of the Word, the worship service is incomplete.

Jesus will always be the Cornerstone of our worship; He is the Living Word of God:

> In the beginning was the Word, and the Word was with God, and the Word was God. He was with God in the beginning. All things were created through Him, and apart from Him not one thing was created that has been created. (John 1:1–3)

Our understanding of who Jesus is and what He has done is determined by teaching and preaching from the written Word of God. As we grasp the depth of His sacrifice and His promises, our worship expression will increase in consistency and freedom—and our lives will continue to be changed forever.

Read More about It

- The first Lord's Supper: Luke 22:14–20
- Instructions regarding the Lord's Supper: 1 Corinthians 11:17–34

The Going Out

The worship service concludes with the Going Out. This is a crucial part of the worship service during which *we* now precede the Word of God out into the world in which we live.

We have separated ourselves for a time to receive the table and the Word. Now it is time for us to take that Word back into our homes, schools, offices, and neighborhoods. We often sing as we go. We also pray as we go. We have been reminded of the great blessing and favor God has brought in our lives, and now it's time to take His presence everywhere we go. We are the body of Christ and the light unto the world:

> *"You are the light of the world. A city situated on a hill cannot be hidden. No one lights a lamp and puts it under a basket, but rather on a lampstand, and it gives light for all who are in the house. In the same way, let your light shine before men, so that they may see your good works and give glory to your Father in heaven." (Matt. 5:14–16)*

During these four key parts of the worship service, we experience many biblical elements of worship—prayer, praise, thanksgiving, charity/giving, confession, preaching and teaching, and Scripture reading, to name a few. All of these are appropriate and necessary elements of the worship service, which you most likely experience on a regular basis. But there is one other central expression of worship that, although it may not be a regular part of the weekly worship service, can never be overlooked: baptism!

Baptism: A Central Expression of Worship

No other worship expression of the church captures the essence of our Christian journey quite like baptism. It is indeed the visible demonstration of the grace gift of salvation and the "great exchange"—our total immersion into the life of Jesus that He has given in exchange for our life of sin. Baptism should be a time of great joy, celebration, and worship.

Not long ago, my coauthor Stan told me about one of the most amazing worship services I've ever heard of, and baptism was the focus. Stan and his wife, Sue, stood for more than five hours one Sunday morning—worshipping, watching, and rejoicing as more than four hundred people entered the waters of baptism! The room was simply electric with the presence of the Lord, as you can imagine.

Individuals, couples, and entire families made a public declaration that day—their lives had been immersed with Christ, and all things were new! I grew up with somber baptism services, and Stan's description helped to reinforce the reality that baptism is an act of exuberant and joy-filled worship. "Listen in" as he describes the experience:

> The singers and musicians surrounded the pool. They sang, they cheered, and they led us all in worship as we witnessed this unique worship expression of so many people. Those who entered the water that day came with great expectation and joy as they symbolically left their old sin patterns, addictions, and failures "dead" in the pool that day.
>
> Words could never describe the effects of our collision of faith and expectation with the power of the Holy Spirit at work in the sanctuary that day. Those four hundred dear saints had a revelation of who God is and what He has done—and nothing could stop them from expressing their deep gratitude to God as they experienced baptism. And as they honored God with their lives, we were all changed.

> ## Read More about It
>
> - John the Baptist baptizes in the wilderness: Luke 3:1–6
> - Jesus is baptized: Matthew 3:13–17
> - Buried and raised with Christ: Romans 6:1–4;
>   Colossians 2:11–15

Call to Worship

After reading this amazing account of the baptism service, don't you want to stop and worship God for the gift of your own salvation? I know I do!

You see, there really is a Redeemer. He is holy and just, faithful and true. He has given us everything we need for life and godliness, and it cost Him life itself. He has given us the freedom to respond to His great grace by exchanging our flawed and failed lives for His life of liberty and victory over sin and death!

We are the redeemed, and God's love and sacrifice for us know no limits. Once we truly understand this, there should be no limit to our expression of worship. He alone is worthy!

Reflections

- There are four basic or key parts of the worship service:

  1. *The Coming In:* This is the time when we literally and figuratively set ourselves apart from the world.
  2. *The Table of the Lord:* This is a visible reminder of God's sacrifice in Jesus Christ that brings our entire focus back to Him, inspiring further worship and proclamation of His gospel.
  3. *The Proclamation of the Word:* This is when teaching and preaching from the written Word of God helps us to grasp the depth of Jesus' sacrifice and His promises to those who believe.
  4. *The Going Out:* This is when we take the proclaimed Word into our homes, schools, offices, and neighborhoods, taking the presence of God everywhere we go.

- Baptism is the visible demonstration of the grace gift of salvation and the "great exchange"—our total immersion into the life of Jesus that He has given in exchange for our life of sin. It is a time for great joy and worship.
- There is no limit to God's love—and there should be no limit to our expression of worship in response!

Prayer

Lord, forgive us when we make the elements of our worship into rituals of religion. Help us see the holiness of these expressions of worship and bring our heartfelt praise before You. Amen.

30

An Everyday Expression

We worship God by serving Him in our everyday
lives with reverence and awe.

As we have emphasized throughout this book, worship is to be a
lifestyle, not just our expression in our corporate assemblies. The
apostle Paul understood this clearly because he lived a life of worship
and service, as these words in his letter to the Romans indicate:

> *For God is my witness, Whom I serve with my [whole] spirit*
> *[rendering priestly and spiritual service] in [preaching] the*
> *Gospel and [telling] the good news of His Son, how*
> *incessantly I always mention you when at my prayers.*
> *(Rom. 1:9 AMP)*

The word *serve* used here is the Greek word *lateuro*, which also
can be translated worship. Paul's ministry itself was an expression of

* **lateuro**—to serve; to worship[1]

worship. It was not something he did because tradition required it. Paul served—worshipped—because he had a personal revelation of God.

You probably know the story well—Paul had an amazing encounter with God on the road to Damascus that changed his life completely. At the time his name was actually Saul, and he was one of the most notable persecutors of Christians in his day. But on the road to Damascus, he received a firsthand view of God's overwhelming power, grace, and mercy. This encounter ultimately changed the entire direction of his life:

> As he traveled and was nearing Damascus, a light from heaven suddenly flashed around him. Falling to the ground, he heard a voice saying to him, "Saul, Saul, why are you persecuting Me?"
> "Who are You, Lord?" he said.
> "I am Jesus, whom you are persecuting," He replied.
> (Acts 9:3–5)

In that moment, Saul (later named Paul) received a revelation of God—of who He is and what He has done—and his life would never be the same. Having been blinded by the light, Saul made his way to Damascus; and there God opened his eyes—not only to see the world around him, but also to see the ministry to which he would devote the rest of his life.

As we know, Paul paid a great price for his worship and service of the Lord Jesus. Yet as his revelation of God grew throughout the years, Paul responded with more and more worship and service. Paul knew the hopeless condition from which God had rescued him—he had a clear revelation of who God is and what God had done in his life—and he was determined to live a lifestyle of worship and service.

Worshipping with Godly Fear, Reverent Awe, and Expectation

We in the Gentile world continue to benefit from Paul's courageous lifestyle of worship, and we can respond to God's revelation with equal fervor and dramatic results in our own lives. When we worship the Lord, we have the privilege of responding to His greatness and to the grace God expressed when He reached down to us in love. And as we worship, we can expect His presence to be revealed.

Although God is our loving Father and our Friend—which He has demonstrated to us through the suffering and the shed blood of His

Son, Christ Jesus—we should never worship Him without godly fear and reverent awe, acknowledging the overwhelming power and glory of His presence:

> Therefore, since we are receiving a kingdom that cannot be shaken, let us hold on to grace. By it, we may serve God acceptably with reverence and awe; for our God is a consuming fire. (Heb. 12:28–29)

God is a good God, and He wants to hear your voice proclaiming adoration, appreciation, desperation, and expectation. He wants that voice to be expressed every day, demonstrating a lifestyle of worship—a life that is being transformed by His Word.

As we draw near to God, we must come with a pure heart in response to who He is and what He has done. Words and actions that fit the worship mold but come from hearts that are not surrendered to God are offered in vain.

However, when we come with words of praise offered from hearts that are fully surrendered to God's truth, we can count on God to respond, and the cycle is complete: God initiates, we respond, and He responds to our worship with His glorious presence!

> "These people honor Me with their lips, but their heart is far from Me. They worship Me in vain, teaching as doctrines the commands of men." (Matt. 15:8–9)

Call to Worship

A personal testimony—such as Paul's testimony and the testimonies of his traveling companions—is a powerful tool with great purpose in God's hands. If you have never had an "intense" encounter with God, you still have a story—a testimony—to share. Whether it is intense or less dramatic, any encounter with God can be equally powerful when it is freely shared with others. Serving others and sharing your story with them as you live your life day by day is an expression of worship.

There have been many occasions when I have shared a personal testimony only to have someone come up after the service and say, "I'm going through the same thing right now. God used your testimony to encourage me tonight." No song that was sung or message preached had that impact—it was the power of the personal testimony that worked in someone's life.

When you and I hold back the testimony of God's work in our lives, we are robbing people around us from being blessed and encouraged. God wants us to share what He has done for us!

Reflections

- The Greek word *lateuro* used for *serve* in the Bible includes both service and worship. Worship involves service.
- We must worship God with reverence and godly fear—He is the greater One and we are the lesser.
- God wants to hear every expression of adoration, appreciation, desperation, and expectation!
- Worship that is lip service only is worship that is in vain.

Prayer

Father, thank You for working in our lives. Lord,
help Your people give testimony to Your greatness
so that others can be blessed. Amen.

Notes

1. Ron Owens and Henry T. Blackaby, *Worship: Believers Experiencing God* (Nashville: LifeWay Press, 2001).

PRESENCE

Song of Worship

"You Are Near"

In awe of You we worship,
And stand amazed at Your great love.
We're changed from glory to glory.
We set our hearts on You our God

Now Your presence fills this place.
Be exalted in our praise.

As we worship I believe You are near.

Blessing and honor and glory and power
Forever forever

31

In God's Presence

Each of us was **created** by God for relationship with Him, but we can only enjoy that relationship by God's **grace**. God's great **love** for us, demonstrated in Christ Jesus, initiates our **response**. The only reasonable and adequate response is our **expression** of worship. As we worship, God has promised His **presence**.

God has promised to be present when we worship.

There really is nothing quite like being in God's presence. According to the dictionary, *presence* means "being present or existing now, not absent, nearness."[1] God's presence is proof that He exists and is always with us. Another word commonly used when referring to God's presence is *manifest,* which means "obvious and undoubted."[2] When God's presence is manifest, it is unmistakable and undeniable! There is no doubt that He exists and is present at that moment.

Three Dimensions of God's Presence

Jack Hayford is a renowned Christian leader who has led worship and taught on the subject of worship for more than fifty years. In his book *Manifest Presence: Expecting a Visitation of God's Presence through Worship*, he offers this insight:

> The Bible reveals at least three different dimensions by which God makes His presence known. Indeed, He is everywhere! But the ways He chooses to manifest Himself imply certain distinctions. Consider: God's awesome presence, God's abiding presence, and God's amazing presence.[3]

Of course, these three dimensions of God's presence are not exhaustive, but they can help us begin to understand the meaning and benefit of being in God's presence. As Blackaby and King write in *Experiencing God*, the first step to experiencing God in our lives is to understand that He is at work around us all the time. So as we examine these three dimensions of God's presence, see if you can relate them to specific parts of your life today.

God's Awesome Presence

God's awesome presence is often described as God's omnipresence, which means that God is present in all places at the same time. This dimension of God's presence is undeniable. King David made perhaps the most concise and compelling statement about the awesome presence of God in Psalm 139:

> *Where can I go to escape Your Spirit?*
> *Where can I flee from Your presence?*
> *If I go up to heaven, You are there;*
> *if I make my bed in Sheol, You are there. (vv. 7–8)*

Likewise, the apostle Paul gave a great picture of the awesome omnipresence of God as he helped the people of Athens identify the true identify of their "unknown god":

> *Then Paul stood in the middle of the Areopagus and said:*
> *"Men of Athens! I see that you are extremely religious in*
> *every respect. For as I was passing through and observing*
> *the objects of your worship, I even found an altar on which*
> *was inscribed:*

TO AN UNKNOWN GOD.

Therefore, what you worship in ignorance, this I proclaim to you. The God who made the world and everything in it—He is Lord of heaven and earth and does not live in shrines made by hands. . . . From one man He has made every nation of men to live all over the earth . . . so that they might seek God, and perhaps they might reach out and find Him, though He is not far from each one of us. For in Him we live and move and exist." (Acts 17:22–24, 26–28)

God is indeed everywhere. The Bible explains that God is just and considers everything we say and do. God's awesome presence surrounds us all the days of our lives—and nothing escapes His notice.

God's awesome presence is simply a fact. God is everywhere at all times, whether we have a relationship with Him or not. Even to those who do not acknowledge God, it is a reality—our God is an awesome God!

All things are naked and exposed to the eyes of Him to whom we must give an account. (Heb. 4:13)

"I tell you that on the day of judgment people will have to account for every careless word they speak. For by your words you will be acquitted, and by your words you will be condemned." (Matt. 12:36–37)

God's Abiding Presence

God's abiding presence is evidenced by God's loving, tender, understanding, warm, and intimate relationship with those who call upon Him as Lord. The Bible tells us again and again of God's abiding presence. Consider these few examples:

"I will never leave you or forsake you." (Heb. 13:5)

"I am with you always." (Matt. 28:20)

"The one who has My commands and keeps them is the one who loves Me. And the one who loves Me will be loved by My Father. I also will love him and will reveal Myself to him." (John 14:21)

God's presence is an abiding—a lasting and enduring—help in time of need *and* in times of great victory. Again, King David's words bring God's abiding presence to life for us:

Where can I go to escape Your Spirit?
Where can I flee from Your presence?
If I go up to heaven, You are there; if I make my bed in
Sheol, You are there.
If I live at the eastern horizon or settle at the western
limits, even there Your hand will lead me; Your right hand will
hold on to me.
If I say, "Surely the darkness will hide me, and the light
around me will become night"—even the darkness is not
dark to You.
The night shines like the day; darkness and light are
alike to You. (Ps. 139:7–12)

God is very serious about abiding with us in an intimate relationship. And we have been given the privilege of responding by abiding in Him. Jesus made it very clear: if we abide, remain, dwell in Him, we will bear fruit and glorify God—we will prove ourselves to be His disciples.

"Remain in Me, and I in you. Just as a branch is unable
to produce fruit by itself unless it remains on the vine, so
neither can you unless you remain in Me.
"I am the vine; you are the branches. The one who
remains in Me and I in him produces much fruit, because you
can do nothing without Me. . . . My Father is glorified by this:
that you produce much fruit and prove to be My disciples."
(John 15:4–5, 8)

It is truly a divine mystery that God Himself would choose to dwell in us, but it is a fact. God continues to invite human beings like you and me to receive Him and enjoy His abiding presence. It is always a matter of choice!

God wanted to make known to those among the Gentiles
the glorious wealth of this mystery, which is Christ in you, the
hope of glory. (Col. 1:27)

God's Amazing Presence

God's amazing presence—sometimes called His manifest presence— is God's response to His followers as they call out for His intervention.

Which of us hasn't cried out to God at some time in our lives? The leaders of the first church in Acts depended on God's unmistakable intervention. Their very lives depended on God's amazing presence, as this passage from the book of Acts reveals:

"Master, You are the One who made the heaven, the earth, and the sea, and everything in them. . . . And now, Lord, . . . grant that Your slaves may speak Your message with complete boldness, while You stretch out Your hand for healing, signs, and wonders to be performed through the name of Your holy Servant Jesus." When they had prayed, the place where they were assembled was shaken, and they were all filled with the Holy Spirit and began to speak God's message with boldness. (Acts 4:24, 29–31)

Most of us in the church today don't face the life-and-death persecution that these dear saints faced every day, but many around the world still do. As the kingdom of God presses into every corner of the globe, missionaries—much like those in the early church—know the reality of their heartfelt need for God's amazing presence to deliver them from evil and to confirm His power to those who desperately need a Savior.

Throughout this book we have read about many people—people living today as well as Bible heroes who lived long ago—who have worshipped God and encountered His amazing presence. From Abraham to Nehemiah to Mary, from me to my wife, Teresa, to the individuals whose stories we've shared with you, God's amazing presence is a proven reality.

Yes, God's amazing presence is still available today. As we worship, we can expect Him to respond. God always delights in the praises of His people. We have every reason to expect God to respond as we worship.

God Is *Always* Present

Recently I found myself in a familiar place—sitting in an auditorium waiting for my son Lee and the rest of the choir to take the stage. Like most choirs, Lee and his fellow university students had been working diligently on their program, and now was the moment of truth!

As the choir made its way to the platform, I could see Lee scanning the audience, looking for Dad. I remembered Lee's first choir program as a three-year-old. I was there then, as well, along with all the other proud papas.

All these years later, so much had changed, and yet nothing had changed. My son was still looking for the approving presence of his father. Lee probably didn't want me to notice that he was looking for me, but I did. And it filled my heart with joy to catch his eye just as I did when he was three—letting him know that yes, indeed, ol' Dad was right there watching and cheering him on as he sang with all his heart.

Call to Worship

The Bible makes it clear that God is doing the same thing every time we come to worship Him. He has promised to be there, and if we will focus our attention on the One who made us, we will find Him in the audience. He loves it when we look for Him. And He loves to hear our voices of praise!

Reflections

- God's presence is proof that He exists and is always with us.
- When God's presence is manifest, it is unmistakable and undeniable.
- There are at least three dimensions by which God makes His presence known:

  1. God's *awesome presence* is often called His omnipresence. He is present in all places at the same time.
  2. God's *abiding presence* is evidenced by God's loving, intimate relationship with those who call upon Him as Lord.
  3. God's *amazing presence* is God's response to His followers as they call out for His unmistakable intervention.

- As we worship, we can come with expectation that God will be there.
- God loves to hear our voices of praise.

Prayer

Lord, thank You for the promise of Your presence when we gather to worship You. Help us to look for the ways You will express Your power among us in our worship. Amen.

Notes

1. Dorling Kindersley, *POCKET English Dictionary* (DK Publishing, 1997).
2. Ibid.
3. Jack W. Hayford, *Manifest Presence* (Grand Rapids, MI: Chosen Books, a division of Baker Books, 2005).

32

God's Presence in the Old Testament

God revealed His presence in Old Testament times in many different ways.

As the Scriptures demonstrate, God has manifested His presence in many different ways since the beginning of time. In this chapter we will consider some of the ways God made His presence known in the Old Testament, and next we will turn our attention to the New Testament.

Though the number of times and ways God manifested His presence in the Old Testament is too great for us to cover in one session, let us explore just a few examples together.

Old Testament Expressions of God's Presence

God was present before the heavens and the earth existed.

In the beginning God created the heavens and the earth. (Gen. 1:1)

God Almighty, the Creator of *everything*, existed before *anything* ever existed. In this age of computer-generated graphics and video games, that concept is not as hard to grasp as it once was. If a graphic designer can "think it," he or she can "create it." That's essentially what happened in Genesis 1:1. God was there, and He brought everything we know into existence.

God was present with Adam and Eve in the garden of Eden.

Then the man and his wife heard the sound of the LORD God walking in the garden at the time of the evening breeze, and they hid themselves from the LORD God among the trees of the garden. (Gen. 3:8)

Adam and Eve knew God. But instead of worshipping God for who He was and what He had done in their lives, they chose to disobey His clear direction, which would have enabled them to have the perfect life on earth. As a result, sin entered the world through their trespass:

"No! You will not die," the serpent said to the woman. "In fact, God knows that when you eat it your eyes will be opened and you will be like God, knowing good and evil." Then the woman saw that the tree was good for food and delightful to look at, and that it was desirable for obtaining wisdom. So she took some of its fruit and ate it; she also gave some to her husband, who was with her, and he ate it. (Gen. 3:4–6)

Therefore, just as sin entered the world through one man, and death through sin, in this way death spread to all men, because all sinned. (Rom. 5:12)

Adam and Eve's response to the Lord's presence in the garden indicates that their revelation of God was complete:

So the LORD God called out to the man and said to him, "Where are you?" And he said, "I heard You in the garden, and I was afraid because I was naked, so I hid." (Gen. 3:9–10)

Like Adam and Eve, we have been given a clear revelation of who God is, who we are relative to who He is, how we should respond, and what we can expect. Instead of bowing before the Lord in repentance and worshipping God for His great redemptive power, Adam and Eve hid from His very presence—from the very One who could redeem them from the sin they ushered into the world. Let's not make the same mistake!

God makes His presence known through His creation.

From the creation of the world His invisible attributes, that is, His eternal power and divine nature, have been clearly seen, being understood through what He has made. As a result, people are without excuse. (Rom. 1:20)

Although the gospel message is being preached around the world today, that wasn't always true. Nevertheless, God has always been "visible" to man through His creation. When God made the earth and all that it contains, He created a reality that testifies of His greatness to every generation of men and women who have lived or ever will live on the earth.

God's presence was in the cloud and pillar of fire that led the Israelites in the wilderness.

The LORD went ahead of them in a pillar of cloud to lead them on their way during the day and in a pillar of fire to give them light at night, so that they could travel day or night. (Exod. 13:21)

Before Jesus came to mediate between God and fallen man, God interacted with His people and their leaders in some amazing ways. The unseen God made a way to lead His people to freedom in spite of their sin and rebellion. Evidently they could not respond to His intervention and leadership without a direct encounter.

Aren't you glad that we have a direct relationship with God today? I know I am!

God revealed His presence to Moses in the burning bush.

Then the Angel of the LORD appeared to him in a flame of fire within a bush. . . . When the LORD saw that he had gone over to look, God called out to him from the bush. (Exod. 3:2, 4)

Can you imagine walking down the street in your neighborhood and encountering a burning bush? It most certainly would get your attention! God was determined to relate to His people, no matter what it took. Moses had the faith necessary to respond to the unseen God.

Even when God does something extraordinary to get our attention, it still takes faith to "hear" Him.

God was present in a cloud at the dedication of the temple.

The trumpeters and singers joined together to praise and thank the LORD with one voice. They raised their voices, accompanied by trumpets, cymbals, and musical instruments, in praise to the LORD:
"For He is good;
His faithful love endures forever;"
the temple, the LORD's temple, was filled with a cloud. And because of the cloud, the priests were not able to continue ministering, for the glory of the LORD filled God's temple. (2 Chron. 5:13–14)

Can you imagine what that worship service must have been like? Surely the leaders and the congregation prepared for months, if not years. This was the crowning moment for the years of dedicated work in building God's place of residence.

Just picture for a moment all the Levites and priests in their finest clothing, fulfilling their duties after months of rehearsal—and God brought the whole ceremony to a screaming halt! His presence was undeniable.

That is the same "presence" that God wants to bring to our assemblies today—and our worship invites Him in!

God was present with Shadrach, Meshach, and Abednego

Read More about It

- King Nebuchadnezzar built a golden statue: Daniel 3:1–7
- The scheme against Shadrach, Meshach, and Abednego: Daniel 3:8–15
- Refusal to worship the statue: Daniel 3:16–18
- Thrown into the fiery furnace: Daniel 3:19–23
- Delivered from the fiery furnace: Daniel 3:20–27
- Nebuchadnezzar praised God: Daniel 3:28–30

in the fiery furnace.

> *Then King Nebuchadnezzar jumped up in alarm. He said to his advisers, "Didn't we throw three men, bound, into the fire?"*
>
> *"Yes, of course, Your Majesty," they replied to the king. He exclaimed, "Look! I see four men, not tied, walking around in the fire unharmed; and the fourth looks like a son of the gods." (Dan. 3:24–25)*

When God intervenes supernaturally, it's really hard to deny. Even an ungodly and self-serving leader like Nebuchadnezzar recognized the presence of God. There is no limit to God's desire to rescue His beloved—and we, too, are the object of His great love!

God was present in the holy of holies inside the temple.

> *The LORD said to Moses: "Tell your brother Aaron that he may not come whenever he wants into the holy place behind the veil in front of the mercy seat on the ark or else he will die, because I appear in the cloud above the mercy seat. (Lev. 16:2)*

As we have discussed previously, God has always been present. God existed before the foundation of the earth was laid—in fact, He spoke all of reality into existence. However, as we also have explored, man was disqualified from direct contact with God because of sin. There simply was no way that unholy man could encounter the one true holy God and survive direct contact, as this verse from Leviticus makes clear. Yet even with the self-imposed limitation of God's holiness, God made His presence undeniable.

> *The heavens were made by the word of the LORD, and all the stars, by the breath of His mouth. . . . For He spoke, and it came into being; He commanded, and it came into existence. (Ps. 33:6, 9)*
>
> *Therefore, just as sin entered the world through one man, and death through sin, in this way death spread to all men, because all sinned. (Rom. 5:12)*

From Virtual Reality to Reality

Perhaps a contemporary term can help us understand how God tried to communicate with His people in Old Testament days. In our computer-driven world, *virtual reality* is a familiar term. It describes our technological ability to experience and interact with events, characters, and situations through a computer-simulated sensory environment.

Similarly God loved His people so much that He revealed Himself through sensory experiences—images and sounds with which they could interact for guidance and instruction. Why? Because without Jesus, our great High Priest, any contact more direct than that would have been fatal!

> • **virtual reality**—a computer-simulated environment that creates a sensory experience involving images and sound

Yes, God was the "ultimate" in virtual reality throughout the Old Testament. God manifested His presence as He willed in order to impact His chosen people and reveal Himself to the ungodly. God wanted His people to have a clear revelation of Him and to respond with worship, and sometimes they did. Unfortunately they didn't always respond to God's visitation—His virtual reality—with repentance, obedience, and ensuing righteousness.

Even so, God wanted an intimate relationship with His people— and still does! After all, He created man and woman for relationship. He walked in the garden right in their midst. He spoke to them face to face. His great desire always has been—and always will be—for us to be together in harmony. Yet the problem remained: unrighteous people cannot be in the presence of a perfectly righteous God.

Virtual reality just wasn't enough. *But God . . . !* But God, who is gracious and merciful beyond our comprehension, knew exactly what to do. He was about to move from *virtual reality* to *reality*. He was about to send Himself in the form of a flesh-and-blood Savior. Jesus—the Way, the Truth, and the Life; the full and complete image of God—was about to come to the earth!

Call to Worship

Have you ever experienced an unusual "encounter" with God? You may not have seen a burning bush or followed a cloud to your destination, but you may have an inspiring story of God's unusual direction or intervention in your life.

I encourage you to share that story with those around you. Your testimony of God's faithfulness may be a key to helping those around you overcome obstacles they are facing (Rev. 12:10–11). Your personal revelation of God's intervention in your life may be the key to revelation for someone you know. And remember, worship *is* our response to God's revelation!

Reflections

- God revealed His presence in a variety of ways throughout the Old Testament.
- God did not speak directly to His people—He spoke through prophets, priests, and kings.
- No one was righteous enough to look into God's face.
- God has always desired to have an intimate, unbroken relationship with us—and He planned from the foundation of the world to make a way for this to be possible.

Prayer

God, You are holy and awesome. Thank You for speaking to us through Your word and Your presence. Give us ways to respond that bring glory to Your name. Amen.

33

God's Presence
in the New Testament

*God revealed Himself in New Testament times
through Jesus Christ and the Holy Spirit.*

God has always desired a people who could dwell in His presence, but mankind was disqualified through disobedience in the garden. Dwelling in the presence of God Almighty always requires complete righteousness.

Something had to be done, and God took the initiative once again. God's people needed His *real, personal,* and *tangible* presence. God desired relationship with mankind so much that He came to the earth in human form to make a way for us to have an eternal covenant relationship with Him—not a covenant sealed by the blood of sheep and goats, but a covenant sealed forever with the blood of the Lamb, Jesus Christ:

> *Now the Messiah has appeared, high priest of the good things that have come. In the greater and more perfect tabernacle not made with hands (that is, not of this creation), He entered the holy of holies once for all, not by the blood*

195

*of goats and calves, but by His own blood, having obtained
eternal redemption. For if the blood of goats and bulls and
the ashes of a heifer sprinkling those who are defiled, sanctify
for the purification of the flesh, how much more will the blood
of the Messiah, who through the eternal Spirit offered Himself
without blemish to God, cleanse our consciences from dead
works to serve the living God? (Heb. 9:11–14)*

Now, that is *reality*!

From the very beginning of time, our God existed—Father, Son,
and Holy Spirit. These three in one are the God who made man in
God's image:

*Then God said, "Let Us make man in Our image, according to
Our likeness." (Gen. 1:26)*

The plan for the creation of man and the salvation of those who
believe was set in motion long before Jesus came to the earth. Jesus
came in the form of man, fulfilled His destiny, and returned to His
rightful place in heaven, but He did not leave us alone. The Holy Spirit
remains with us today to carry out God's will in each of our lives. The
Spirit of the Living God provides for us every moment of every day.
Now that's revelation worthy of worship!

New Testament Expressions of God's Presence

**Jesus was the Word of God who physically dwelt on the
earth.**

*The Word became flesh and took up residence among us.
We observed His glory, the glory as the One and Only Son
from the Father, full of grace and truth. (John 1:14)*

It is a fact of history: Jesus of Nazareth came to Earth and lived as
a man. He felt what we feel, and He experienced every temptation we
will ever know:

*Therefore since we have a great high priest who has passed
through the heavens—Jesus the Son of God—let us hold fast
to the confession. For we do not have a high priest who is
unable to sympathize with our weaknesses, but One who has
been tested in every way as we are, yet without sin.
(Heb. 4:14–15)*

Our God became real flesh and blood to make it possible for us to be re-qualified for His presence.

Jesus was and is the exact image of God, for He *was and is* God.

> [Now] He is the exact likeness of the unseen God [the visible representation of the invisible]; He is the Firstborn of all creation. For it was in Him that all things were created, in heaven and on earth, things seen and things unseen, whether thrones, dominions, rulers, or authorities; all things were created and exist through Him [by His service, intervention] and in and for Him. And He Himself existed before all things, and in Him all things consist (cohere, are held together). (Col. 1:15–17 AMP)

From the creation of the earth, the stage was set for God's entry through Jesus Christ. God knew exactly what it would take for man to respond to His love: Jesus. He is the full revelation of God!

> "But you," He asked them, "who do you say that I am?"
> Simon Peter answered, "You are the Messiah, the Son of the living God!"
> And Jesus responded, "Simon son of Jonah, you are blessed because flesh and blood did not reveal this to you, but My Father in heaven. (Matt. 16:15–17)

Jesus' life and words gave testimony of God.

> "The One who sent Me is with Me. He has not left Me alone, because I always do what pleases Him." (John 8:29)

When we examine the love that Jesus demonstrated in word and deed—the mighty signs and wonders that He performed—there is simply no doubt that He was God. God is love, and only God could love us enough to die for our sins.

Jesus and God are one and the same.

> "The Father and I are one." (John 10:30)

> "The one who has seen Me has seen the Father." (John 14:9)

There is simply no doubt: Jesus was and is God. While on the earth, Jesus demonstrated the very life of God—only doing and saying as the

Father directed. His communion and communication with God were complete—He was and is God!

> So Jesus said to them, "When you lift up the Son of Man, then you will know that I am He, and that I do nothing on My own. But just as the Father taught Me, I say these things." (John 8:28)

Jesus sent the Holy Spirit to remain with us.

> "Nevertheless, I am telling you the truth. It is for your benefit that I go away, because if I don't go away the Counselor will not come to you. If I go, I will send Him to you. When He comes, He will convict the world about sin, righteousness, and judgment." (John 16:7–8)

We all understand the principle of giving to receive, and Jesus embodied that truth. He knew that His presence as a man was only a foreshadowing of God's desire to intervene in our lives. Jesus had to depart the earth, but He did not leave us or forsake us.

> "I will not leave you as orphans; I am coming to you." (John 14:18)

The Holy Spirit came upon and empowered His people, and He is present in us.

> "But you will receive power when the Holy Spirit has come upon you, and you will be My witnesses in Jerusalem, in all Judea and Samaria, and to the ends of the earth." (Acts 1:8)
>
> God wanted to make known to those among the Gentiles the glorious wealth of this mystery, which is Christ in you, the hope of glory. (Col. 1:27)

The Holy Spirit enables us to experience God's presence and be in relationship with God. And He operates through us to impact the world around us. That is what experiencing God is all about—the Holy Spirit invites us to join Him as He works! He really is alive and well on planet Earth, dwelling in and among His people. We *are* the body of Christ.

Made to Enjoy God's Presence

We were made to enjoy God's presence both now and throughout eternity. God has given us the invitation and the means—Christ *in* us, the hope of glory—to do just that. Our part is to live our lives by faith, fully expecting that we *will* encounter God's manifest presence.

We experience God's presence as we respond to His great love and surrender our lives to Him. Surrender involves presenting all our members and faculties as a living sacrifice, as instructed by Romans 12:1. I like the way the Amplified Bible describes a living sacrifice: holy, devoted, consecrated, and well pleasing to God. This, we are told, is our reasonable—rational and intelligent—act of service and spiritual worship.

> I APPEAL to you therefore, brethren, and beg of you in view of [all] the mercies of God, to make a decisive dedication of your bodies [presenting all your members and faculties] as a living sacrifice, holy (devoted, consecrated) and well pleasing to God, which is your reasonable (rational, intelligent) service and spiritual worship. (Rom. 12:1 AMP)

As we come before God in worship with surrendered and expectant hearts, He *will* respond, making His amazing presence known to us. God was present in the beginning, and He is present with us now. He is, of course, worthy of our worship and adoration. Here is a list of biblical elements of what should be a regular part of our lives and worship.

- Expectation (Pss. 27:14; 62:5; Isa. 8:17; 40:31)
- Obedience (Jer. 7:23; 42:6; Titus 3:1; Heb. 5:9)
- Sacrifice (Pss. 51:16–17; 54:6; 116:17; Matt. 9:13; Rom. 12:1)
- Faith (Matt. 17:20; 21:21–22; Rom. 3:28; 5:1–2; Eph 2:8–9; Heb. 11)
- Patience (Luke 8:15; 2 Thess. 3:6; James 1:4; 5:10–11)
- Thanksgiving (Pss. 50:14; 95:2; 100:4; 107:22; Phil. 4:6)
- Attention (Prov. 4:20; 5:1; 7:24; 1 Tim. 4:13)
- Submission (James 4:7; 1 Peter 2:13–17; 5:5)
- Prayer (Matt. 6:5–6; 6:9-13; 14:23; 26:41; Rom. 8:26; 1 Thess. 5:17)
- Meditating on God's Word (Josh. 1:8; Pss. 63:6; 119:15, 148; Phil. 4:8)
- Humility (Col. 3:12; Titus 3:1–2; 1 Peter 5:5)
- Surrender (Rom. 6:13–14; 12:1; Phil. 3:8–10)
- Drawing near (Ps. 73:28; Heb. 10:19–22; James 4:8)

- Listening (Pss. 78:1–4; 81:13; Prov. 8:32; 19:20; Eccles. 5:1)
- Watching (Matt. 25:13; Mark 13:35–37; 14:38; Luke 21:36; Acts 20:28–31; 1 Cor. 16:13; 1 Thess. 5:6; Rev. 3:3)

Call to Worship

I encourage you to focus on any element on the preceding list that has captured your attention (and there may be more than one). Your particular interest in any one element may be the Lord drawing you into a deeper worship experience. Take the time to examine each related Scripture carefully. God deeply desires to speak to you personally as you study His Word!

Reflections

- God revealed Himself in New Testament times through Jesus Christ and the Holy Spirit.
- Jesus is the express image of the invisible God.
- Jesus—the Way, the Truth, and the Life—is the only way we can approach a holy God.
- Jesus sent the Holy Spirit to be with us and dwell within us.
- The Holy Spirit enables us to experience God's presence and be in relationship with God.
- As we come before God in worship with surrendered and expectant hearts, He makes His presence known to us.

Prayer

Lord, thank You for Your Spirit that dwells within my heart.
Lord, let me be sensitive to Your presence and responsive
to all You want me to do for Your glory. Amen.

34

Encountering God's Presence Today

We can encounter God's presence today when we worship.

We have seen that God made Himself known in a variety of ways in Old Testament times. Then, in the days of the New Testament, God makes His presence known through His Son, Jesus Christ, and until now through the Holy Spirit. The Scriptures also tell us that God is fully and forever present in heaven, and one day we will know what it is like to experience God's presence face to face. But what about *today*? How do we encounter God's presence right here and now?

In chapter 31, we explored three dimensions of God's presence: God's awesome, abiding, and amazing presence. We experience all three of these dimensions of God's presence at various times and in various ways.

God's awesome presence is with us every day, moment by moment, whether we realize it or not. God is indeed everywhere at all times. We also can experience God's abiding presence daily. God has promised to dwell with us and in us, and God's Word is always true. It's up to us to make a daily decision to abide, remain, and dwell in Him. This decision leads to an intimate relationship with God and a fruitful life that glorifies Him. And, finally, there are many ways we can experience the responsive, intervening nature of God's amazing presence—*often in the midst of worship!*

Encountering God's Amazing Presence

I have shared the story about my encounter with God's amazing presence at a Promise Keepers event when I was surrounded by more than 60,000 men. God reached out and touched me as if I were the only person in the entire stadium that day. Of course, I knew others had to be encountering God's presence in a powerful way, too, and I was correct.

My coauthor, Stan, told me about a friend of his who had an amazing encounter with God at the very same event. Stan and his wife, Sue, were having dinner with their friends Tom and Celina Martinez when Tom told the story of this encounter that had changed his life.

Tom grew up believing in God, but like so many of us, he drifted away and began living for himself. The choices he had made in life were costing him his marriage, his family, and all the things he held so dear.

Some friends invited Tom to attend the same Promise Keepers event that I attended, and in spite of his spiritual condition at the time, he accepted. Though he didn't know it, Tom was about to encounter the manifest presence of God—and his life was about to change forever.

As the men traveled across two states together, the van was filled with praise and worship music. Tom had never seen grown men so excited and filled with expectation. God was using their expectation to set Tom's encounter in motion, because "coming with expectation" is crucial to experiencing God in worship.

When these fifteen friends entered the stadium to join the sixty thousand men in worship, the presence of God was overwhelming. As so many men have commented through the years, the sense of God's presence is very real at these events. A stadium full of men worshipping together is truly an unforgettable experience.

Within minutes, in the midst of worship, Tom was face to face with the One who had created him and who loves him with an everlasting love. He thrust his hands in the air and received Jesus as Lord and Savior. Even through the tears of repentance and joy, the old Tom tried to drag him back to "reality." After all, what was he thinking? And how could he act like this in front of all these macho guys?

Then God sealed the deal. As Tom opened his eyes, all he could see was thousands of men around him in the same condition—worshipping, surrendering, repenting, and crying out in adoration and desperation for the One they always longed to encounter.

Worship was the key! And God was present. God truly inhabits the praises of His people. And when God is present, even "macho sinners" like Tom find themselves responding.

God's Amazing Presence Is Available to All

Since that day twelve years ago when Tom encountered the amazing and overwhelming presence of God in worship, Tom's marriage and family have been restored. Today he and his wife, Celina, are intercessory prayer leaders who serve regularly in one of the most dynamic churches in the country.

Even though we have never met, Tom and I forever will be linked by our Promise Keepers encounter. I'm certain that Tom and I were not the only ones who were deeply impacted by God's amazing presence that day, and I look forward to hearing story after story around the throne of God one day. God is truly worthy of our praise!

God's amazing presence is available to *all* who surrender their lives to Him. As we learn to live by faith with a full expectation that God will respond, He will do just that. He is ready to meet *you* right now as you worship Him.

But where do you start?

The other day as I was approaching my office door at LifeWay, I caught myself doing the craziest thing. I had pulled out my car keys with the automatic remote lock on my key ring and there I was—walking toward my office door trying to unlock it with my car key remote! I looked around to see if anyone saw me, and to my relief no one was there. I found my office key and unlocked the door, but then I started laughing so hard at myself that people came out of their offices to see what I was laughing at! I enjoyed telling on myself the rest of day!

The Bible tells us the key that opens up the gate of God's court is thanksgiving and praise. Trying to open His gate with a musical style or some type of religious ritual makes about as much sense as trying to open your office door with your car remote. It just doesn't work. Psalm 100:4 says, "Enter His gates with thanksgiving and His courts with praise." The next time you desire a worship connection with God just start giving Him thanks. Just start naming all He has done for you—your life, your health, your family, your salvation, and so on. It won't be long until you are in the court of praise experiencing His awesome presence and power.

Call to Worship

Coming to worship with expectation that God will indeed be present is crucial. As we know, God inhabits our praise *and* He is a rewarder of those who diligently seek Him.

> But You are holy, enthroned on the praises of Israel. (Ps. 22:3)
>
> Now without faith it is impossible to please God, for the one who draws near to Him must believe that He exists and rewards those who seek Him. (Heb. 11:6)

Is your worship different when you have the expectation of encountering God? I know mine is. God always gives us a choice to seek Him. He is always available, but He will not pressure us to respond. It is up to us to desire an encounter with the Living God in a tangible and undeniable way.

Are you content with your worship experience as it is currently? If not, make a point to come to worship with expectation that He will meet you there. Ask God for a fresh encounter with His amazing presence. Then, worship Him with faith-filled expectation, and He will respond!

Reflections

- We encounter God's awesome, abiding, and amazing presence at various times and in various ways.
- We often encounter God's amazing presence as we worship.
- We can and should come before God with the expectation that God will meet us as we worship.
- When God is present, lives are always changed.
- God's presence always invites our response of worship.

Prayer

Lord Jesus, I come to Your gate with a heart full of thanksgiving. You have done so much for me. I thank You and I fall before You to give You my praise. Amen.

35

Faith Is Foundational to Worship

The key that unlocks the door.

Faith fills us with expectation and prompts us to take action, being confident that God will respond. This was true in the days of the Old and New Testaments, and it is true today. And we know that we can come before God with faith-filled expectation because God has promised to reward those who believe that He exists and who diligently pursue Him.

> *Now without faith it is impossible to please God, for the one who draws near to Him must believe that He exists and rewards those who seek Him. (Heb. 11:6)*

Before the fall Adam and Eve had every reason to expect good things from God. They were qualified to dwell in His presence. There was no barrier between them and God because sin had not yet entered the world.

Then, because of their disobedience, Adam and Eve—and all their offspring, from generation to generation—were disqualified from God's presence. As we have underscored, a righteous God can never dwell in the presence of unrighteousness.

But the good news is that we have been requalified because of Jesus' sacrifice. *The only way we can come into God's presence is through Jesus the Christ.* Receiving salvation through Jesus by faith—and faith alone—fulfills the complete requirement of the law. We have been redeemed (purchased) and justified (made right with God) by the blood of the Lamb. Our "right standing" with God gives us every right and every reason to worship God with the faith-filled expectation that He will respond.

So, by faith we come before God to worship Him for who He is and what He has done. Our worship makes a place for us to encounter God's manifest presence. And when God is present, our lives are changed!

Faith—the Sure Foundation

Faith, then, is foundational to worship—and to *all* of Christian life. Just consider the role of faith in the process of the Christian journey.

It is by faith that we surrender our lives to the saving grace and lordship of Jesus Christ and choose to remain or abide in Him continually.

> *For by grace you are saved through faith, and this is not from yourselves; it is God's gift—not from works, so that no one can boast. (Eph. 2:8–9)*

> *"I am the vine; you are the branches. The one who remains in Me and I in him produces much fruit, because you can do nothing without Me." (John 15:5)*

It is by faith that we choose to be different from the world and to receive God's truth so that we may be transformed.

> *Do not be conformed to this age, but be transformed by the renewing of your mind, so that you may discern what is the good, pleasing, and perfect will of God. (Rom. 12:2)*

It is by faith that we believe and act upon God's promises.

So don't throw away your confidence, which has a great
reward. For you need endurance, so that after you have done
God's will, you may receive what was promised.
"For in yet a very little while,
the Coming One will come and not delay.
But My righteous one will live by faith; and if he draws
back, My soul has no pleasure in him." (Heb. 10:35–38)
In the same way faith, if it doesn't have works, is dead by
itself. (James 2:17)

And as we act upon God's promises by faith, we receive
the promises of God in our lives!

Therefore, ridding yourselves of all moral filth and evil
excess, humbly receive the implanted word, which is able to
save you. . . . But the one who looks intently into the perfect
law of freedom and perseveres in it, and is not a forgetful
hearer but a doer who acts—this person will be blessed in
what he does. (James 1:21, 25)

This is the Christian life—receiving and believing the Word of
God and allowing that Word to transform us more and more into His
likeness. Our revelation of God's greatness and His desire to make a
way for us to live abundantly on this earth is the key to our lifestyle of
worship.

What Faith Is

The Bible gives us an excellent definition of faith:

Now faith is the reality of what is hoped for, the proof of what
is not seen. (Heb. 11:1)

Faith is essential, but faith is possible only where there is hope—
hope that comes from relationship with God. As you read and meditate
on God's written Word, hope will abound in you. God is the God of
hope, and you can abound in hope by the power of the Holy Spirit. If
you are struggling with your faith today, these verses from the book of
Romans are for you:

For whatever was written before was written for our
instruction, so that through our endurance and through the

*encouragement of the Scriptures we may have hope. . . .
Now may the God of hope fill you with all joy and peace in
believing, so that you may overflow with hope by the power
of the Holy Spirit. (15:4, 13)*

*This hope does not disappoint, because God's love has been
poured out in our hearts through the Holy Spirit who was
given to us. (5:5)*

What Faith Does

The Bible also tells us what faith does:

*For by grace you are **saved** through faith . . . it is God's gift.
(Eph. 2:8, emphasis added)*

*The law, then, was our guardian until Christ, so that we could
be **justified** by faith. (Gal. 3:24, emphasis added)*

Faith allows us access to God and all that He desires for us. As we
have seen, flesh and blood cannot reveal the truth of God; only the
Spirit of God leads us into all truth. God has given us the ability to live
by faith, but it is up to us to put our God-given faith into action.

How We Obtain Faith

Once again, we can look to the Bible for specific instruction
regarding how we obtain faith:

*So then faith comes by hearing, and hearing by the word of
God. (Rom. 10:17 NKJV)*

Have you ever wondered what your life would be like if you had
not heard about Jesus and your need for faith in Him? The Bible is very
clear: faith comes by *hearing*. That's why preaching and teaching the
Word of God, and then proclaiming His love for and to every person on
the earth, are so important. As we worship God, even unbelievers can
be drawn to know more about this wonderful Savior we serve.

*"In the same way, let your light shine before men, so that
they may see your good works and give glory to your Father
in heaven." (Matt. 5:16)*

The Results of Faith

According to the Word of God, faith provides salvation, peace, hope, power, grace, and so much more. And faith is the foundation to which we add those things that are necessary to make us fruitful throughout our lives on the earth:

> For this very reason, make every effort to supplement your faith with goodness, goodness with knowledge, knowledge with self-control, self-control with endurance, endurance with godliness, godliness with brotherly affection, and brotherly affection with love. For if these qualities are yours and are increasing, they will keep you from being useless or unfruitful in the knowledge of our Lord Jesus Christ. (2 Pet. 1:5–8)

Through no decision of our own, we were born into a life of sin. We were born with a sin nature. No matter how good we are, we all fall short of perfection:

> For all have sinned and fall short of the glory of God. (Rom. 3:23)

But through our faith in Jesus Christ, we have been made completely new:

> Therefore if anyone is in Christ, there is a new creation; old things have passed away, and look, new things have come. (2 Cor. 5:17)

As a result, we are completely worthy of God's presence, now and for eternity.

Faith allows us to know God, fellowship in His presence, and receive the blessings He has promised. God truly is a rewarder of those who diligently seek Him!

The Requirements of Faith

We cannot experience the results of faith unless we meet the requirements of faith. The Bible tells us:

> In the same way faith, if it doesn't have works, is dead by itself. (James 2:17)
> We walk by faith, not by sight. (2 Cor. 5:7)

We are saved by faith and faith alone, but faith without corresponding action is like being able to breathe and choosing not to take a breath! It is in the implementation of our faith—the actions we take by faith in our daily lives—that we discover who we are in Christ. This is a core message of Blackaby and King's *Experiencing God:* we experience God in our lives as we respond to Him with *faith and action.*

> Therefore . . . let us lay aside every weight and the sin that so easily ensnares us, and run with endurance the race that lies before us, keeping our eyes on Jesus, the source and perfecter of our faith. (Heb. 12:1–2)

Worship—Our Faith in Action

Our freedom in the Christian life *and* in worship is totally dependent on faith. As we put action to our faith, God has promised to reward us. In worship, we put action to our faith by lifting our voices in praise, and God rewards us with His presence.

Call to Worship

As you worship, remember that your worth is not an issue if you have surrendered your life to God. He is worthy of your praise, and you are able to worship God because His righteousness has been placed in you—by faith. God simply wants your full attention and your complete surrender.

You don't need to be perfect to enter the King's presence. All you need is to have faith that God is who He says He is, and to make a place for Him to come and meet with you. God *desires* to inhabit your worship.

He is the One who is high and lifted up. He is the One who is worthy of all praise. There is nothing like the awesome, abiding, and amazing presence of the Lord. In His presence, all things are possible!

Reflections

- We must have faith if we want to encounter God's presence.
- Faith is foundational to worship and to all of Christian life.
- God rewards those who diligently seek Him.
- We can expect God to be present as we worship Him.

- Our worship begins with surrendering our lives to God through faith in Jesus Christ.
- We can come to God and worship Him only through faith in Jesus Christ. There is no other way.
- Faith comes by hearing (and reading) the Word of God.
- As we act upon God's Word by faith, we receive God's promises in our lives.
- Faith without action is "dead"—useless.

Prayer

Lord, I know that even the faith I have comes from You. As I read Your Word, let my faith grow. And as my faith grows, work in my life so that I will express faith-filled worship every day. Amen.

EXPERIENCE

Song of Worship

"Prepare the Way"

Prepare the way,
Make straight the path for Him.
Let the King of Glory enter in
Let the King of Glory enter in.
Who is this King of Glory?

(Chorus)
The Lord strong and mighty,
The Lord mighty to save.
The earth is full of His glory,
Creation calls prepare the way.

His love endureth forever
His power is without an end
His strength is victory's treasure
Let all who call His name prepare the way.

WORDS AND MUSIC BY JARED ANDERSON
©2004 VERTICAL WORSHIP SONGS/ASCAP
C/O INTEGRITY MEDIA, INC., 1000 CODY ROAD, MOBILE, AL 36695

36

Experiencing God in Worship

Each of us was **created** by God for relationship with Him, but we can only enjoy that relationship by God's **grace**. God's great **love** for us, demonstrated in Christ Jesus, initiates our **response**. The only reasonable and adequate response is our **expression** of worship. As we worship, God has promised His **presence**. We can always **experience** God in worship!

When we experience God in worship, we are empowered to serve Him—and worship Him more.

As Blackaby and King explain in *Experiencing God*, each time the Lord invites us to become involved with Him as He works through us, we must overcome every obstacle with faith and action. Experiencing

God in worship requires *faith* and *action* as well. Our revelation of God should always elicit our response; and as we have seen, complete surrender through a life of worship and service is indeed our only reasonable and adequate response to who God is and what He has done.

> *I appeal to you therefore, brethren, and beg of you in view of [all] the mercies of God, to make a decisive dedication of your bodies [presenting all your members and faculties] as a living sacrifice, holy (devoted, consecrated) and well pleasing to God, which is your reasonable (rational, intelligent) service and spiritual worship. (Rom. 12:1 AMP)*

The Story of the Seventy

I have always loved the story of the Seventy—the group of disciples who were chosen by Jesus—as recorded in Luke 10. In many ways they represent a perfect picture of faith-filled worship in response to God's revelation. These precious disciples definitely *lived* a life of worship. They spent day after day listening to, observing, and following Jesus' instructions and example. They sat at the Master's feet, and when He invited them to make a difference in their world, they responded!

> *After this, the Lord appointed 70 others, and He sent them ahead of Him in pairs to every town and place where He Himself was about to go. (Luke 10:1)*

The Seventy were not the culturally elite of that day; nor were they likely theologians and scholars. They were just ordinary people like you and me. In fact, not even one of their names is mentioned in the Bible. Most likely, their only real qualification for service at that moment was their eager desire to spend time with Jesus.

I can just imagine the crowds of people who came and went as Jesus walked through the towns and villages in those days. Multitudes often followed Jesus as He fulfilled the Father's desire for His life. But the Seventy were special to Him—they were followers who just wouldn't go away.

Can you imagine what it must have been like for them? They were constantly in the presence of God Himself. They had set aside all the other agendas of life in order to sit at the feet of the Master, absorb His every word, and serve Him no matter what the cost. They were experiencing God in worship *every* day.

When it came time for Jesus to proceed toward His human destiny—Jerusalem and the cross—they were the ones He chose to go and announce that He was coming:

> "Now go; I'm sending you out like lambs among wolves.
> Don't carry a money-bag, traveling bag, or sandals; don't
> greet anyone along the road.
> "When you enter any town, and they welcome you,
> eat the things set before you. Heal the sick who are there,
> and tell them, 'The kingdom of God has come near you.'"
> (Luke 10:3–4, 8–9)

All they had to do was go to the places Jesus sent them, follow His explicit instructions in the process, proclaim that the kingdom was near, and put their faith into action in order to see God's intervention in many, many lives. And in the process, these Seventy—these ordinary people just like you and me—experienced God in amazing ways:

> The Seventy returned with joy, saying, "Lord, even the
> demons submit to us in Your name." He said to them,
> "I watched Satan fall from heaven like a lightning flash.
> However, . . . rejoice that your names are written in heaven."
> (Luke 10:17–18, 20)

The Seventy must have learned unlimited valuable principles during the time they had spent at Jesus' feet; and when it was time to put their faith to work, they were empowered by His presence. These ordinary people got a firsthand view of God's willingness to respond to their act of *lateuro*!

* **lateuro**—to serve; to worship

Call to Worship

So, although the principles that the Seventy had learned at the feet of Jesus were important, what they really needed to fulfill their mission was God's presence; and they experienced God's presence as they served and worshipped. The Seventy proved their faith by their actions, and their reward was great: they experienced God's presence and power. And so can we!

Reflections

- The Seventy from Luke 10 were given explicit instructions and a clear purpose by the Lord, and they experienced God as they responded to His invitation.
- When we go where God sends us, obey His instructions, and put our faith into action through worship and service, we experience God's presence and power in amazing ways.
- God always responds when we serve and worship Him.
- We prove our faith by our actions—and experience God in the process.

Prayer

Father, thank You for using ordinary people to do Your extraordinary work. May I be one of those people who trust You enough to allow You to work through my life in extraordinary ways. Amen.

37

Keys for Worship

Experiencing God in worship requires time and sacrifice.

When Jesus offered a truly God-sized assignment, the Seventy were ready to step out in faith and serve God. They responded to their revelation of God on Earth by offering their lives as living sacrifices. They had adopted a worship *lifestyle*, and Jesus was honored and well pleased. We can do the same thing today as we respond to God's revelation of who He is and what He has done in our own lives.

There are four simple yet profound keys to experiencing God in worship, and the story of the Seventy gives us a clear pattern to follow. We will consider the first two keys now and look at the other two in chapter 38.

Key #1: Time in God's Presence Is Time Well Spent!

Experiencing God in worship starts with our willingness to give God first place in our lives. This means spending time with Him every day—through prayer and devotion to God's written Word and God's Living Word. As we have seen, God rewards those who diligently seek

Him. Apart from Him, we truly can do nothing—and that includes worship.

Jesus set the example for us. He was continually getting away from the crowds and distractions and spending time with the Father. While the crowds pressed in for His attention, Jesus knew the source of His strength—time with the Father:

> But the news about Him spread even more, and large crowds would come together to hear Him and to be healed of their sicknesses. Yet He often withdrew to deserted places and prayed. (Luke 5:15–16)
>
> Very early in the morning, while it was still dark, He got up, went out, and made His way to a deserted place. And He was praying there. (Mark 1:35)

Time with the Father is always time well spent! We too must develop a hunger for God that supersedes our desire for the things of the world. We can't receive a fresh revelation of God and the continual infilling of the Holy Spirit without intentionally changing our priorities in life.

The apostle Paul gives us these instructions:

> Look carefully then how you walk! Live purposefully and worthily and accurately, not as the unwise and witless, but as wise (sensible, intelligent people), making the very most of the time [buying up each opportunity], because the days are evil. Therefore do not be vague and thoughtless and foolish, but understanding and firmly grasping what the will of the Lord is. And do not get drunk with wine, for that is debauchery; but ever be filled and stimulated with the [Holy] Spirit. (Eph. 5:15–18 AMP)

The only way we can know the will of the Lord and be filled with the Holy Spirit is to spend time in God's presence. This is the first key to experiencing God in worship. Following the example of the Seventy, we must spend time in the presence of God if we are to receive revelation. That is what the Seventy did first and foremost: they spent time with Jesus. As we do this, worship becomes our natural response—and the priority of our lives. Here are some possible opportunities or times for you to spend time with Jesus.

- As you study the Bible
- As you pray
- When you first wake in the morning, before you are distracted
- Right before you fall asleep at night
- While you are driving
- While you enjoy a favorite activity—alone or with others (hiking, cooking, boating, visiting with friends, etc.)
- As you serve others

Key #2: Count the Cost

The story of the Seventy actually begins in Luke 9. That's when Jesus' ministry took a major turn:

> *When the days were coming to a close for Him to be taken up, He determined to journey to Jerusalem. (Luke 9:51)*

Until this time, Jesus had been setting the stage for His triumphant moment on the cross. He was the Lamb who would be slain to take away the sins of the world. There had always been a cross in His future, and the time had come for that climactic victory.

Jesus knew the road He was about to travel was the most difficult one anyone had ever known. He knew the cross would cost Him great suffering and death, but the time had come—the sacrifice had to be made. The world needed a risen Savior.

As Jesus made clear His plans to go to the cross, many of His followers declared their desire to go with Him, no matter what. Jesus responded by teaching them about the cost of discipleship:

> *As they were traveling on the road someone said to Him, "I will follow You wherever You go!" . . . Then He said to another, "Follow Me."*
> *"Lord," he said, "first let me go bury my father." . . . Another also said, "I will follow You, Lord, but first let me go and say good-bye to those at my house."*
> *But Jesus said to him, "No one, who puts his hand to the plow and looks back is fit for the kingdom of God."*
> *(Luke 9:57, 59, 61–62)*

Jesus wanted those disciples to fully understand that the cost of following Him toward His destiny was real and measurable. The cost included persecution, rejection by friends and family members, inconvenience, and material loss. In the language of that day, the concept of burying one's father implied waiting until the father died so that the son could claim his inheritance. Jesus knew, however, that a far greater inheritance awaited them as they stepped out in faith and followed Him—the same inheritance that awaits us today.

The Seventy followed and served Jesus—worshipped Him—at great cost to themselves. They gave up their time, their families, their earthly goods, and their own agendas to go and declare that the kingdom was near. The New Testament is filled with examples of the loss and rejection believers experienced, yet they willingly suffered loss that others might know Christ. And they were greatly rewarded. The writer of the book of Hebrews provides a clear picture of the cost these faithful believers endured as they followed Jesus:

> *Remember the earlier days when, after you had been enlightened, you endured a hard struggle with sufferings. Sometimes you were publicly exposed to taunts and afflictions, and at other times you were companions of those who were treated that way. For you sympathized with the prisoners and accepted with joy the confiscation of your possessions, knowing that you yourselves have a better and enduring possession. So don't throw away your confidence, which has a great reward. For you need endurance, so that after you have done God's will, you may receive what was promised. (Heb. 10:32–36)*

Following Jesus required sacrifice then, and it requires sacrifice today. There are countless stories of ordinary people who have counted the cost and said "Yes!" to God's invitation that I could share with you. However, I want you to focus on your own story.

Perhaps you already know what it's like to spend time in God's presence, hear God's invitation to join Him as He works, and respond—and possibly you don't always realize that is what is happening.

For every Sunday school teacher, for every choir member, for every home group leader, for every person who invests even one hour in doing missions work or encouraging a friend—there remains a great reward. Recognizing and responding to God's call takes so many different forms. And every response requires faith and obedience. Every response is indeed an expression of worship (*lateuro*).

Perhaps God is using this book to stir your heart to action, or greater action, on His behalf. If so, then may I remind you that this stirring is God inviting you to join Him as He works right where you are!

Your response to His invitation will allow you to continue to experience God in your life. Worship Him as you step out in faith, my dear friend. He is worthy. And He is waiting.

God used my son Lee one Saturday morning to give me a powerful example of trust. We were driving back from Tyler, Texas, where Lee was an alternate to audition for the All State choir. Lee and I have always enjoyed "hanging out" together, and this day had been no different. But I had something huge on my mind to discuss with him, and finally the moment was right so I went for it.

For the next hundred miles I told him that LifeWay was interested in me as the potential Director for LifeWay Worship. They asked me to indicate my willingness to be considered for the responsibility by the following Monday—just two days away. I explained to Lee that I understood how big an impact such a change would have on him. He was a junior, well established in his school and all set for an awesome senior year. I remember saying it this way: "There are sixteen million Southern Baptists and everyone of them put together don't mean as much to me as you do—if you say you can't do it, I'll call them Monday and turn down their request and we'll never look back." What Lee said next was straight from God and one of the real early indications that God was at work and leading me to LifeWay. Lee said "Well, Dad, I don't see any way God's will for your life would hurt me. If you will do God's will, then it will work out fine for me."

Lee had expressed not only trust in me but trust in God to take care of him. There is one thing I was totally right about that day. The move we made to Nashville did impact Lee's life in a profound way including where he is in college and what he is studying today. God has proven to both of us that what Lee said that day was totally true. We can follow where God leads us and worship Him because our heavenly Father can be trusted.

Call to Worship

Jesus asked the Seventy to step out in faith and proclaim the coming of the Savior of the world. That sounds like an enviable role to us today, but the cost to them was potentially severe. God wants to invite *you* to join Him as He works, as well. And His invitation will require faith and action on your part.

Are you ready to step out in faith and enter into *lateuro*—worship and service—right now? Responding to His invitation is always the first step to experiencing God in worship!

Reflections

- Spending time in God's presence each day is the first key to experiencing God in worship.
- To receive a fresh revelation of God and the continual infilling of the Holy Spirit, we must intentionally change our priorities in life.
- Joining God as He works is costly.
- Following Jesus can cost us our time, material possessions, reputation, agendas, health/safety, and even our lives. Yet we will be rewarded for our sacrifice.
- A great inheritance awaits us as we step out in faith and follow Jesus!

Prayer

Lord, I know following You will bring me to decisions of trust and sacrifice. Give me the grace to trust You even when I don't understand. Amen.

38

More Keys for Worship

*Experiencing God in worship requires us to trust
and obey and keep our focus on Jesus.*

It is important to remember that *the Seventy were ordinary people*, just like you and me. When talking about the Seventy, the Bible never mentions they had great oratory skills or natural charisma. However, it is clear that they spent time in God's presence, and their obedience makes clear that they were prepared to pay the cost of following His instructions.

God was at work around the Seventy. He was about to invite them to join Him in His work and experience Him in their own lives.

Key #3: Trust and Obey

As we rejoin the Seventy in Luke 10, they are about to be sent on the journey of a lifetime. They are about to be thrust into a God-sized assignment. They are about to experience God in ways they could not have possibly imagined!

Jesus gives the Seventy specific instructions about where to go and how to respond as they step out in faith:

> *"Now go; I'm sending you out like lambs among wolves. Don't carry a money-bag, traveling bag, or sandals; don't greet anyone along the road. . . . When you enter any town, and they don't welcome you, go out into its streets and say, 'We are wiping off as a witness against you even the dust of your town that clings to our feet.'" (Luke 10:3–4, 10–11)*

The Seventy chose to respond, and they fulfilled their destiny. They really were just like us—simple, ordinary people—yet they were destined to walk in the full revelation of God's grace and power on the earth; destined to be transformed into the image of Jesus; destined to spend eternity with the One who loves them with an everlasting love.

God still uses ordinary people who are willing to do His work in His way in the places He sends them. We simply cannot fear people or the consequences of our obedience. Joining God as He works through us always requires faith and obedience.

The words that you see on every page of this book are living proof that God uses ordinary people who are willing to trust and obey. My friend and coauthor, Stan Moser, heard the Lord clearly invite him to develop this study in the midst of a business meeting at LifeWay several years ago.

Stan is a businessman with a lifetime of success as an executive in the Christian music industry. Until God invited Stan to join Him as He developed this message on worship, Stan had no clue that he was also a writer and a teacher. It took great faith, trust, and obedience for him to step out and say, "Yes, I'll write this book by Your grace," and you are holding the result of literally years of trust and obedience on his part.

You can do the same in your own life. God doesn't simply use preachers, worship leaders, and celebrities to accomplish His work on this earth. He is constantly working around you, too. As you respond to His invitation to join in, He will use you in ways that you can't even imagine right now!

> *Now to Him who is able to do above and beyond all that we ask or think—according to the power that works in you—to Him be glory in the church and in Christ Jesus to all generations, forever and ever. Amen. (Eph. 3:20–21)*

Key #4: Remember That It's All about Jesus.

As we've noted previously, the Seventy experienced God in the midst of their service and worship in amazing ways. They responded to their time in Jesus' presence with great obedience, and they saw sickness and oppression flee in their wake. Can you imagine what that must have been like?

When they returned to the Master, they were obviously excited and filled with awe, wonder, and joy. As they overcame their own crisis of belief—which we can assume they surely must have experienced—and stepped out in faith, they did indeed experience God. Many lives were changed as a result, including their own, for this life and all of eternity:

> The Seventy returned with joy, saying, "Lord, even the demons submit to us in Your name."
> He said to them, "I watched Satan fall from heaven like a lightning flash. Look, I have given you the authority to trample on snakes and scorpions and over all the power of the enemy; nothing will ever harm you. However, don't rejoice that the spirits submit to you, but rejoice that your names are written in heaven." (Luke 10:17–20)

Of course, they could accomplish nothing apart from Jesus and the power of His name. Likewise, we can accomplish nothing apart from Him. That's why His promise to meet us as we worship is so crucial. In His presence, all our enemies, all our distractions, all our doubts and fears and difficult circumstances must bow. He is the true King of kings. And when the King is present, all things are possible!

> "I am the vine; you are the branches. The one who remains in Me and I in him produces much fruit, because you can do nothing without Me." (John 15:5)

Authentic service and worship must *always* be about Jesus! Yet, just like the Seventy, we can be quickly tempted to move from total dependence on Jesus as we're worshipping and serving to dependence on our own abilities. This is a particular danger for those who serve in church leadership and possess great personal charisma. As God moves in our midst, it is so easy for us to trust in our own talents and abilities rather than maintain total dependence on God. It is crucial that Jesus remains the object, source, and fulfillment of our worship. He truly deserves the glory!

Instructions for Our Mission

Jesus gave the Seventy very specific instructions, and they had to follow those instructions in order to be successful in their mission. We, too, have encountered many instructions during our study together. Each of these instructions requires us to be obedient and to keep our focus on Jesus as we live a lifestyle of worship. Our aim should always be to satisfy and please Him.

> *No soldier when in service gets entangled in the enterprises of [civilian] life; his aim is to satisfy and please the one who enlisted him. (2 Tim. 2:4 AMP)*

Call to Worship

It is our heart's desire that this book has increased your revelation of who God is and what He has done in your life. And as you respond to that revelation with worship, your life will be changed forever!

The Word of God is always our guide—showing us His desire and direction for every part of our lives. Take the time to read the verses below and let them settle into your heart. The King of Glory is about to enter in like never before, if you will invite Him. Your worship *is* that invitation!

> *[Jesus] answered: "'Love the Lord your God with all your heart, with all your soul, with all your strength, and with all your mind'; and 'your neighbor as yourself.'" (Luke 10:27)*

> *"I give you a new commandment: love one another. Just as I have loved you, you must also love one another. By this all people will know that you are My disciples, if you have love for one another." (John 13:34–35)*

> *"The one who has My commands and keeps them is the one who loves Me. And the one who loves Me will be loved by My Father. I also will love him and will reveal Myself to him." (John 14:21)*

> *"No one has greater love than this, that someone would lay down his life for his friends. You are My friends if you do what I command you." (John 15:13–14)*

Do not be conformed to this age, but be transformed by the renewing of your mind, so that you may discern what is the good, pleasing, and perfect will of God. (Rom. 12:2)

For Christ's love compels us, since we have reached this conclusion: if One died for all, then all died. And He died for all so that those who live should no longer live for themselves, but for the One who died for them and was raised. (2 Cor. 5:14–15)

Therefore, God's chosen ones, holy and loved, put on heartfelt compassion, kindness, humility, gentleness, and patience, accepting one another and forgiving one another if anyone has a complaint against another. Just as the Lord has forgiven you, so also you must forgive. (Col. 3:12–13)

Above all, put on love—the perfect bond of unity. And let the peace of the Messiah, to which you were also called in one body, control your hearts. Be thankful. (Col. 3:14–15)

Let the message about the Messiah dwell richly among you, teaching and admonishing one another in all wisdom, and singing psalms, hymns, and spiritual songs, with gratitude in your hearts to God. And whatever you do, in word or in deed, do everything in the name of the Lord Jesus, giving thanks to God the Father through Him. (Col. 3:16–17)

Therefore, brothers, since we have boldness to enter the sanctuary through the blood of Jesus, by the new and living way that He has inaugurated for us, through the curtain (that is, His flesh); and since we have a great high priest over the house of God, let us draw near with a true heart in full assurance of faith, our hearts sprinkled clean from an evil conscience and our bodies washed in pure water. (Heb. 10:19–22)

Now without faith it is impossible to please God, for the one who draws near to Him must believe that He exists and rewards those who seek Him. (Heb. 11:6)

Therefore, since we are receiving a kingdom that cannot be shaken, let us hold on to grace. By it, we may serve God acceptably, with reverence and awe; for our God is a consuming fire. (Heb. 12:28–29)

Therefore, ridding yourselves of all moral filth and evil excess, humbly receive the implanted word, which is able to save you. But be doers of the word, and not hearers only, deceiving yourselves. (James 1:21–22)

Dear friends, let us love one another, because love is from God, and everyone who loves has been born of God and knows God. The one who does not love does not know God, because God is love. (1 John 4:7–8)

Reflections

- God uses ordinary people to do God's work in God's way in the places God sends them.
- When we follow Jesus' instructions, we will see great results.
- Joining God as He works through us always requires faith and obedience.
- We can accomplish nothing apart from Christ!
- Authentic worship must always be about Jesus.

Prayer

Lord, as I learn how to worship You, may the focus not be on my worship, but on Your greatness. Amen.

39

Worshipping without Restraint

God's glory is revealed when His people
lose themselves in worship.

In Luke 10:20 Jesus told the Seventy that their names were written in heaven. I wonder if they had any idea what that meant? Jesus had an eternal perspective on their lives. As great as their earthly experience of serving Him and seeing His power expressed through their obedience was, Jesus knew it would not compare with heaven. But there was even more in store for them on Earth. They had responded to God's revelation by joining Him in His work as they fulfilled their mission. Now they were about to experience God, with a glimpse of His glory, as they worshipped the King of kings as He entered Jerusalem:

> *Now He came near the path down the Mount of Olives,*
> *and the whole crowd of the disciples began to praise God*
> *joyfully with a loud voice for all the miracles they had seen:*
> *"Blessed is the King who comes in the name of the*
> *LORD!*

Peace in heaven and glory in the highest heaven!"
(Luke 19:37–38)

Though the Scriptures do not say specifically that the Seventy were part of "the whole multitude of the disciples," it is logical to assume that these devoted followers responded to the once-in-a-lifetime opportunity to worship Jesus as He entered the city to fulfill His destiny.

As Jesus came into the city, the Seventy—and the entire multitude—weren't sitting quietly and waiting for someone to ask them to rise and sing verses one, two, and four! They were shouting, singing, waving palm branches, and running alongside the Savior of the world. Their worship was completely unrestrained. They were proclaiming to all who would listen that the King had arrived, that sins could be forgiven, and that we can live at peace with God as a result. *Now that is experiencing God in worship!*

Revelation, Worship, and God's Presence

The Seventy had spent time with Jesus, and they *knew* He was the Son of God. They *knew* He had come to set the captives free. Jesus was and is the Lamb who was slain to forever provide a way to the Father.

These disciples had a revelation of God and had seen what He had done in their midst, and their response on this day was unrestrained worship. And God Himself fulfilled His promise to be present with them as they worshipped. God always inhabits the praises of His people.

As Jesus entered Jerusalem that day, He came in the midst of His disciples' intense, loud, and unceasing worship. Imagine the scene with me.

Perhaps you are one in the crowd who doesn't really know what's going on, but you sense something amazing is unfolding before your eyes. You can hear the noise of all the people begin to swell. Someone special is coming. You can hear the shouts of praise and acclamation.

Surely it is the king or a member of some royal family. Why else would the people be so unrestrained in their praise and adulation? As you strain to catch a glimpse of this royal moment, you are confronted with true royalty—the High Priest of all time. And He is riding a donkey, just as you have read about in the Holy Scriptures.

"Rejoice greatly, Daughter Zion! Shout in triumph, Daughter Jerusalem!

> See, your King is coming to you; He is righteous and
> victorious,
> humble and riding on a donkey, on a colt, the foal of a
> donkey." (Zech. 9:9)

Now, it's decision time for you. If Jesus really is who they say He is—if He really is the Son of God come to set us free from sin—then you must respond! The worship of His disciples is overwhelming . . .

> "'Blessed is the King who comes in the name of the LORD'
> Peace in heaven and glory in the highest heaven!"
> (Luke 19:38)

Surely it *is* Him! There is no way to stop the worship. The religious leaders have lost control. If the people stop praising Him, the stones will start to cry out. And at that moment you make the decision in your heart: Jesus is Lord! There is none other like Him in all of heaven and earth!

> [Jesus] answered, "I tell you, if they were to keep silent, the
> stones would cry out!" (Luke 19:40)

Your heart has been captured in your moment of revelation, and you lift your voice—your own expression of unhindered worship—in unison with the others, shouting, "Blessed is the King . . . blessed is the King . . . glory in the highest!" God Himself is present, and you will never, ever be the same.

The presence of God in Christ Jesus at that moment provides an indelible living image of God's promise to be present when His people worship Him. God *always* inhabits the praises of His people. And when God is present—when the revelation of God increases—complete and unrestrained worship is our only reasonable response.

As great as this marvelous day was, heaven will be even greater. As we will see in the next section, then we will know Him perfectly and completely and we will give Him perfect and complete worship.

Call to Worship

I pray that these words give you a simple yet profound vision of real worship—worship in response to who God is and what He has done in your life. I often wonder just how different our corporate worship times would be if each service began with a clear proclamation of God's goodness and mercy toward us—*before* the first word of the first hymn or worship chorus was sung.

I encourage you to do that as you begin the next worship service at your church. If not from the platform, at least in your heart, begin to focus on the revelation of God in your life—even as you sing. Then join in with the Seventy and all the precious saints around the throne of God and raise your own expression of worship. You are His beloved child, and He wants to hear your voice of praise and adoration more than you could ever imagine.

Reflections

- Worship is our response to God's revelation of who He is and what He has done.
- Our worship provides a place of meeting with God—He has promised to inhabit our praises.
- The Seventy had a revelation of God Himself, and nothing could stop them from worshipping. We have the same reason to worship today!
- The Seventy worshipped God with their words and actions *without restraint*!
- God *always* inhabits the praises of His people.

Prayer

Father, thank You for the power of Your Word.
As Your people worship You, bring glory to Your name
and not to our worship! Amen.

40

Never-Ending Worship

Our worship invites God's presence, His presence
brings increased revelation, and we respond
with never-ending worship.

Worship is critical to our lives here on planet Earth, and worship is our destiny throughout all eternity. Throughout this book we have seen example after example of God's people responding to Him with worship. Their worship invited the presence of God, and their lives were changed forever.

We also have been given a clear picture of our never-ending worship around the throne of God in heaven. The cycle of worship begins with our response, and it is indeed never-ending. As we learned in chapter 4, worship is continual in heaven as the angels and elders cry out day and night.

> *Each of the four living creatures had six wings; they were*
> *covered with eyes around and inside. Day and night they*
> *never stop, saying:*
> *"Holy, holy, holy,*
> *Lord God Almighty,*
> *who was, who is, and who is coming." (Rev. 4:8)*

There is no shortage of revelation of God's presence in heaven, and the worship never stops. Imagining Jesus' triumphant entry into Jerusalem gives us just a small glimpse of what our eternity will hold. Our response will be worship—the kind of unrestrained worship offered by the crowd gathered on the dusty road outside the city of Jerusalem.

Jesus went to Jerusalem to fulfill His destiny right in the midst of His followers, most likely including the Seventy, and they could not keep silent. They had devoted their lives to Jesus, they had seen Him do mighty deeds through their own obedience, and they had the personal assurance of spending eternity with God. They had every reason to worship the King—and so do we! Never-ending worship was their destiny, and it is ours as well.

We have a lot in common with the Seventy. They were ordinary people who had taken the opportunity to spend time with the Savior, to believe and receive His words of life, and to reach out to those around them who needed to know that the Savior was near. Although Jesus is no longer physically with us, He has provided the Holy Spirit who resides in us and teaches us all things:

> The anointing you received from Him remains in you, and you don't need anyone to teach you. Instead, His anointing teaches you about all things, and is true and is not a lie; just as it has taught you, remain in Him. (1 John 2:27)

Like the Seventy, we have been given a mission. Jesus has called us to go forth into our neighborhoods, schools, churches, and workplaces to declare that the kingdom is near and available. His Holy Spirit empowers us to speak words of love and healing and deliverance to those in need:

> This is how we have come to know love: He laid down His life for us. We should also lay down our lives for our brothers. If anyone has this world's goods and sees his brother in need but shuts off his compassion from him—how can God's love reside in him? Little children, we must not love in word or speech, but in deed and truth. (1 John 3:16–18)

Just like the Seventy, we can fulfill our mission by choosing to spend time in God's presence, responding to His revelation, and making a place of meeting as we worship Him. God's amazing love for us makes it all possible. The cycle of worship is never-ending: He loves us; we respond; He inhabits our response; and we worship even more! God is waiting right now for us. He's always waiting for us to lift our "instruments of praise" to Him.

> The Israelites who were present in Jerusalem observed the Festival of Unleavened Bread seven days with great joy, and the Levites and the priests praised the LORD day after day with loud instruments. (2 Chron. 30:21)

Blowing to the Box

When I think of "loud instruments," I'm reminded of an analogy I heard the late Bob Benson—accomplished businessman, author, and speaker I mentioned before—describe many, many years ago—one that tells about being a band parent. And that brings to mind the many band competitions Teresa and I have enjoyed. His story is so much like our experience, I often tell it in the first person. The profound illustration at the end of Bob's story still inspires many as I tell it across the country wherever I go. So here's my version of the "blow to the box" story much like the way Bob Benson told it many years ago.

We have been band parents ever since my son, Lee, was able to pick up a drum and play. That means that I've been to countless band contests—those all-day events where you are guaranteed to sit in the bleachers somewhere and watch as many as fifty or sixty bands perform their halftime shows for the judges in the press box.

Frankly, it's an exhausting way to spend a Saturday—that is, until *your* band takes the field! At that point, it doesn't matter that you have seen the show a thousand times—the "band parent within" takes over. You may know every note and every step that is coming, but your response cannot be restrained.

As the song comes to its conclusion, the band turns toward you; and in one final moment, they start what is known as "blowing to the box." Every band director throughout all of time teaches the same message: *this is the moment where you blow your instrument with all your heart, soul, and strength.* No matter what instrument you play, as you face the press box, it's time to put your very best performance on the line. Lift your head, blow a little harder, and play a little louder. It's time to let them hear all you have to give.

In Lee's junior year the Creekview High School Band made it to the Texas State Championship at the Alamo Dome in San Antonio.

That's quite an accomplishment for the band of a school so new to this intense competition. The competition of Texas bands is something you cannot imagine if you've never seen it. We were so proud of our band for this remarkable accomplishment.

When the public address speaker announced our band, there we were again: standing on the top row of bleachers, waving our arms in the air, and screaming at the top of our lungs as the Mustang band was "blowing to the box"!

Call to Worship

If you apply the analogy to the Christian experience, the seat you put our heavenly Father in has everything to do with how you will live and worship. If you see Him in the judge's seat in the press box, carefully judging your performance, then you will approach the Father with caution and fear and live without ever knowing the freedom of serving Christ.

But if you can put Him in the Father's seat and see Him on the top row of the bleachers to get a better view of His dear child—as the One who waves His arms and screams His support with all His strength to let you know that He loves you and is there for you—then nothing and no one can keep you from experiencing God at that very moment. You can "blow to the box" as you live for His glory!

Worshipping God in response to who He is and what He has done is a privilege that we simply cannot ignore. We were made for worship, and even now God is waiting for us to respond.

Our God is truly the King of all kings and the Lord of all lords. His name is Jesus, and He's waiting for our response to His revelation! Worship while you wait. Worship while you are under the weight of circumstances. Worship when He seems near and when He seems far away. If you have placed your faith in Christ, your name is written in the Book of Life. And when this life is over, you will be worshipping Him day and night for eternity. Now that's something to celebrate!

You see, worship really is the key to experiencing God. He's ready when you are.

Reflections

- Jesus is present with us all the time through the Holy Spirit.
- The Holy Spirit dwells in us—teaching and guiding us daily.
- Jesus has called us to love one another, and worship empowers us to fulfill this mission.
- Worship is our response to God's revelation of who He is and what He has done.
- Seeing God as a holy and merciful Father who desires our deepest expression of adoration, thanksgiving, appreciation, and expectation sets us free to experience God in worship.

Prayer

Oh God, I want to know You—not just who You are, but who You want to be in my life. I surrender to Your will for me. I want to experience You in worship. I want to serve You with a worshipper's heart. Amen.

Epilogue

I wonder if there will be video in heaven. I can just imagine this vault of videos (high definition of course) with scene after scene of the events described in the Bible. I could check out a volume for a thousand years or so and see for myself what it was really like. I can tell you one of the first ones I want to see: I want to see Nehemiah 8.

Here's a little background before we roll the tape: After fifty-two days of work and completion of the wall, the call went out, and for seven months the exiles returned. Each one was registered by genealogy and the offerings started flowing in. (push PLAY) Nehemiah 8 opens with God's people gathered in front of the Water Gate. In unison they call for Ezra the scribe to bring them the book of the law. The air is charged with electricity as he wipes down the book and carefully opens it. It's been almost ninety years—more than two generations—since God's people have seen, much less heard, anyone read from this book. The anticipation must have been off the chart!

Ezra is standing on the first pulpit mentioned in the Bible, and it was built just for this occasion. There is a hush across the crowd when the book opens and suddenly, spontaneously, God's people rise to their feet. Ezra blesses the name of Jehovah and the people shout together "Amen, Amen!" And then something amazing happens. As he is reading the book, they fall on their faces and weep. They weren't imitating anyone. It had never happened in any of their lifetimes! They were confronted with the character of Holy God expressed in the pages of His law. They realized they were undone before this God of righteousness, and they responded the only way anyone can—they fell prostrate before God.

Then men, appointed to the task and prepared for this moment, explained the law and told all the people to stop their crying. "Go, celebrate a feast! Your strength comes from rejoicing in the Lord!" they declared. The celebration erupted and they enjoyed the greatest feast anyone had ever known before. It must have been amazing. Hit rewind! I want to see it again!

I really would love to see it again. But not just for what happened *then*. I want to see it happen *now*. Why? Because the scene captured in Nehemiah 8 perfectly illustrates what revival in our time could look like. And it's the entire message of *Seven Words of Worship*. I'm convinced a repeat of that scene is exactly what today's church and every Christian need and what we all should pray for today. Basically four things happen in Nehemiah 8 that need to happen now if we want to experience the power of God in lives marked by worship. Here they are:

- The people called for God's Word.
- The man of God read from the Word of God and men of God gave the meaning of it to the people.
- The people listened and responded to God's law with humility and repentance.
- The people worshipped their God with celebration and abandon.

There it is—God's people responding to God's revelation about Himself. And the worship that erupted recast the future of their nation for generations to come. What had been lost was suddenly regained. What had been ignored was now obeyed. The connection with God that had been broken for generations was restored and the joy of His presence was experienced with great effect. The glory of God filled His people and consequently, their world. *Do it again, Lord. Do it again!*

Oh, that the people of God would declare the Word of God in our day! May His church rise up and declare His character to the world we live in—a character of righteousness and holiness, but also a character of grace and love, full of mercy and forgiveness. It will be then, and only then, that we will see real worship that changes lives and redirects generations and nations to the glory of God!

Pour out on us, Oh God! Let us see your greatness! Amen and Amen!

About the Authors

$\mathbf{M}$ike Harland has been in worship ministry for more than twenty-five years. He has served a variety of local churches—from small rural churches to some of the largest mega-churches in America. A native of Corinth, Mississippi, Mike is a graduate of Delta State University and New Orleans Baptist Theological Seminary with a master's degree in church music.

Currently Mike is the Director of LifeWay Worship, a department of LifeWay Christian Resources, a position that enables him to speak, teach, and lead at worship conferences and events nationwide. Prior to joining the LifeWay staff, he served as worship leader and associate pastor of First Baptist Church in Carrollton, Texas.

An accomplished musician and songwriter, Mike has had numerous original songs published throughout his ministry, including "Bow the Knee," "It's Still the Cross," and "Playing Games at the Foot of the Cross" as well as choral works that include "Save in the Cross," "Jesus Our Treasure," and "America, We Must Not Forget." He and his wife, Teresa, reside in Franklin, Tennessee, with their children Lee, Elizabeth, and John.

$\mathbf{S}$tan Moser is a leading worship ministry consultant and president of Spin 360, a subscription-based service providing worship resources for the church. As an executive in the Christian music and publishing industry for more than thirty-eight years, he has held key executive positions at Word Records, Star Song Communications, and Maranatha! Music.

Stan has played a vital role in the development of contemporary Christian music and the contemporary worship movement since their beginnings, helping to launch Andrae Crouch, Evie, the Imperials, Amy Grant, Twila Paris, Petra, Phillips/Craig/& Dean, the Newsboys, and Bill Gaither's Homecoming Series among many others.

Stan is the author of *The Gift of Music . . . or Is It?* (Music and the Word Ministries) and *Great and Precious Promises for Singers and Musicians* (LifeWay). His son, Jackson, attends Tennessee State University and works at Spin 360. Stan and his wife, Sue, live in Brentwood, Tennessee.

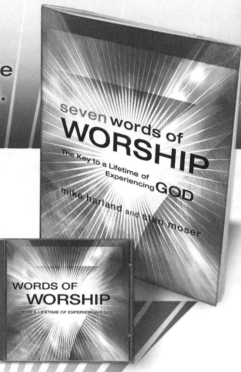